DON'T SETTLE FOR A SEAT

DON'T SETTLE FOR A SEAT

You Don't Belong at the Boys' Table—
It's Time to Join Successful Women
Rewriting the Rules

KARRIE BRADY

LIONCREST
PUBLISHING

DON'T SETTLE FOR A SEAT

You Don't Belong at the Boys' Table—It's Time to Join Successful Women Rewriting the Rules

ISBN   978-1-5445-2275-3 *Hardcover*

978-1-5445-2273-9 *Paperback*

978-1-5445-2274-6 *Ebook*

CONTENTS

INTRODUCTION

I can't just sit here.

The thought was on autorepeat as I lay in bed the first night after I decided to drop out of college and move home. I had been living on my own, renting a one-bedroom house off campus and taking care of myself, without even a roommate to disrupt my independence. I was a nineteen-year-old sophomore studying biomedical engineering, fascinated with human health and hungry for knowledge. I planned to specialize in prosthetics and hoped to work with the Wounded Warriors Project in the future.

All that changed when my dad nearly died in a dirt-bike accident. He was riding on a new practice track and overshot a jump, landing on the ground with the wind knocked out of him and other riders headed his way. Disoriented, he scrambled to get out of their path and rode headfirst off the steep side of the track. Thankfully, he had his protective neck gear on because that was the only reason he made it out of the fifteen-foot drop alive at all. He did, however, have a broken neck that would take almost a year to heal. Even after weeks of bed rest, he would be unable to work, drive, or do simple household tasks for months.

My mom couldn't take care of him herself—as the executive director of a nonprofit, she worked at least sixty hours a week to manage an organization that would fall apart without her. My sister had a kid, my brother was only fourteen, and hiring a stranger to care for my dad was no one's idea of an ideal solution, so there I was. It felt right to be with my family during this crisis, but it certainly wasn't what I expected to happen during one of my first years of adulthood.

A different kind of person might have viewed this as simply a forced sabbatical from college. All I had to do was take care of my dad, and my parents would put a roof over my head and food on the table just like in high school.

But to be honest, it burdened my psyche. Living with my parents after being so independent felt like life in reverse. If I wanted to live under my parents' roof without feeling like a child again, I needed my own money. Settling for a meaningless paycheck seemed like a waste of time, but few other options were available to me—after all, I was just a high school grad with no real work experience other than summertime lifeguarding. Plus, I had to be available whenever my dad needed me, so regular hours were out of the question. What I really needed was total freedom to choose when and how much to work. (I think you know where this is going...)

The answer was to start my own business in the one thing I was interested in and qualified for: fitness. I was already in great shape; I'd played soccer in high school and became a religious workout fiend in college. I hadn't finished my biomedical engineering studies yet, but I probably understood the human body better than the average gym trainer and definitely better than the average trainee, and all I had to do was get certified. Starting a personal training business was the perfect solution for my situation, and I knew it was possible because I could see that the health and fitness industry was blowing up online.

My story, while specific to me, isn't really that special at all. Every entrepreneur starts with the same two ingredients: passion and need. Together, they create the fertile ground where sustainable, life-changing businesses grow.

READY TO START YOUR STORY?

If you have a passion and a need, you're in the right place.

Let me guess: the conversation with the voice in your head

sounds a little like this when you think about striking out on your own and starting a business.

"It would be so perfect to have my own business!" you think.

"But what if it doesn't take off?" your inner critic says.

"I know my idea can work—look, that girl on Instagram is doing it."

"But she's clearly way more experienced. Why would anyone choose me over her?"

"Well, that's not fair. Everyone has to start somewhere, right?"

"Sure, but there are already so many people doing what I want to do. I have no idea how to make people notice me, let alone convince them to pay me!"

"Yikes, maybe I'm not cut out for this..."

I'm not really guessing—that's exactly what went through my mind when I decided to take the plunge, and that's why I'm writing this book. Way too many women let these thoughts convince them not to pursue their business ideas. Worse, some give it a shot but never find the right path and end up with shattered dreams and broken hearts. That voice in our head is a problem, and it took me years to understand the solution. Let me save you some time and heartache (and probably a good chunk of money too).

The skills you need to launch a thriving business are already within you.

You use them every day without even realizing it. You listen to your friend and give her thoughtful advice. You entice your partner to focus on you, and only you. You relentlessly negotiate to get your kids to eat their vegetables. You convince your boss to give you an extra day off. You spend all day connecting with other people, serving their needs, and persuading them to serve yours in return.

Lightbulb moment—that's all business is!

The stereotypes would have us believe otherwise. Business is about competition, transactions, numbers, and greed, right? White men at big tables in skyscrapers, moving millions with a handshake. Cookie-cutter products designed anonymously and made somewhere overseas. Sneaky ads that manipulate us to part with our hard-earned cash.

That's the old way, and it's dying fast. We want to buy products and services we understand, from real people we can trust, and a new generation of internet-powered entrepreneurs is making it happen. The response has been so powerful that even big corporations are changing their ways, recognizing the undeniable truth that people buy through emotional connection.

And here's the best part: women are wired for it because we're biologically and socially predisposed to value personal connection. We're the primary caretakers in our species, the ones who physically birth the next generation and nurture it through its most vulnerable years, and evolution has equipped us to build the unbreakable emotional bonds that make it all possible. On top of that, society still teaches girls to fulfill the role of caretaker—to play nice, share, help others. Men simply aren't primed for personal connection the way we are. In this new business paradigm, where money is made through genuine connection, women are the fittest for survival.

It's as simple as this: your customers have problems, and you have solutions. The tools to make the connection are already in your toolbox. You just need to learn how to use them in new ways.

When I first launched my business, I didn't know any of this. And spoiler alert: I bombed. Hard. I wasted years banging my head against a brick wall, putting more and more effort into the same flawed strategy because I didn't understand what I was doing wrong. Eventually, I gave up, telling myself entrepreneurship just wasn't for me. My story could have ended there, but thankfully, I found the opportunity and the courage to try again. When I finally learned to do it right, I was living my dream life within a year. *One year.* How much pain could I have saved if I had done it right from the start?

You don't need to waste all that time. Instead, you can learn from my mistakes and eventual success. Before you take even one step down this road, we need to tear down the myths and limiting beliefs that will keep you from thriving, and teach you to use the tools already at your disposal. This book will guide you to overcome your fears and build a thriving business by tapping into the feminine instinct to connect and serve.

SECOND TIME'S A CHARM

When I set out to be an online fitness coach at age nineteen, I went all in...and all my worst fears came true. That nagging voice in my head? It was so right. Fitness is a crowded space. Anyone with a nice body and the patience to get through a few months of training (or maybe not) can throw their hat in the ring.

I knew I was a better coach than most. I had a deeper, more scientific understanding of exercise and nutrition, so I knew exactly how to help my clients reach their goals. I truly cared and put in more effort than anyone else I knew, hustling day and night to support my clients and attract new ones. For the first year, I'd be at the gym coaching clients from four-thirty to seven in the morning, come home and do marketing and sales work online while taking care of my dad, then head back to the gym to see more clients after my mom got home from work at six or seven in the evening. Nothing was more important to me than making this business work.

You wouldn't be able to tell at first glance, though, since all that hustle didn't seem to do much good. I consistently struggled to convince people to sign up with me, despite constant outreach on social media, which was so energetically draining. Worse, the clients I did get weren't the kind of clients I was hoping for. In my business fantasies, I worked with dedicated go-getters who showed up on time, gave it their all, and stuck with the program until they reached their fitness goals. In the real world, my clients wanted quick results with minimal effort, and they quit when it didn't happen that way. I spent all my time on my business and gave up everything else, but after two years it still didn't pay the bills.

When I started working a side job to make ends meet, it was the beginning of the end. By then, my dad had recovered, and I'd moved to Las Vegas to live with a friend and see if my business might blossom better there. Sin City disappointed on that front, but it did introduce me to my now-husband. It wasn't long before he and I decided to skip town for Los Angeles, where we both hoped to find better opportunities.

When we made it to LA, my business had about a drop left in

the tank. I felt like a bird stuck on the ground, jumping and flapping and dying to take flight, but I just didn't have the right moves. Our new home was even more expensive, and honestly, the weight of worry and defeat had worn me out. So, I told myself I just wasn't cut out for entrepreneurship, and I let my business grind to a halt. Time to let it go and get a job—my worst fear come true.

A corporate gym hired me as a trainer, which was a relief at first because at least I could eat and pay the rent without going broke and keep working in the same arena I had a passion for. Sound familiar? The charm wore off quickly, though. Every day reminded me of why I'd wanted to start a business on my own in the first place. I was stuck working early mornings and late nights for pay that was barely worth it and way less than what an independent trainer could make. That sucked, but what I hated most was having to meet sales quotas. Whenever a new member joined, we had to either cold call them or just walk up to them on the gym floor and offer personal training. Overall, the process felt pushy and sleazy.

Thankfully, the sheer awfulness of my job kept my entrepreneurial dreams alive in the back of my mind. So, when a fitness influencer posted on Instagram that she was looking for an assistant in LA, I jumped at the opportunity. I was the perfect fit for the job. I knew her brand because I followed her closely and admired her work, and I knew the industry because I'd been working in it for three years. I thought maybe I was meant to support an entrepreneur, not be one, so I ditched the gym for my new gig without a second thought.

That's when I finally learned the truth. It's not that I wasn't cut out for business—I had just been doing everything wrong! I could finally see the inside of a thriving online fitness business, and the revelation blew me away. Her success didn't come from some secret recipe of charisma and social media fairy dust; it came from smart strategies and tactics that I finally felt like I could master. I met my first sales mentor through her circle of colleagues and learned how to sell in an emotional way that worked. Not too long after, my boss moved me from assistant to the sales team, and in six months I sold $150K of her online coaching program. Eventually, she brought me inside the program to teach these same sales strategies to her students as well.

That was the proof that I could do it—I could be a successful entrepreneur. More importantly, I understood what had been getting in my way before. Flawed beliefs were the culprit behind the ineffective strategies that had kept me overworked and underpaid. Everything that needed to change was within me, not *out there* beyond my control. The world might be full of people who didn't believe in me or take me seriously; it always is for people who don't fit the entrepreneur stereotype because of their age, gender, race, or some other reason. But it turned out that the skeptics and haters didn't matter so much once I learned to believe in myself and attract other people who would do the same.

I tried again, at first with fitness coaching, which landed me multiple four-figure deals. But soon, I pivoted to coaching other women how to sell online, which felt like my true passion after realizing what *not* having those skills can do to someone with big dreams.

My goals came to life faster than I ever imagined. I left the gym in 2017, and within a year I felt the weight of money worries lifting from my chest and was traveling in Europe for months at a time. A year after that, my husband and I had our dream wedding. Another year passed, and we bought our dream house in LA. He gets to pursue his passion for acting, and we both get to spend plenty of quality time with our two babies and three rescue dogs. We can afford to travel, hire a nanny, take time off, support our families...we have true freedom.

Most importantly, I LOVE my business. The money is just a by-product of the fact that I wake up every day excited to do what I'm meant to do. I get to live in my strengths because I built my business around them, so I never feel like I'm doing chores or counting the minutes to the end of the workday. I spend most of my time connecting with like-minded people and making a real difference in their lives. Most importantly,

I'm always working toward the goal that lies closest to my heart: putting more money in the hands of women.

HERE'S TO THE DREAMERS

Most of my coaching clients and online course students are women who have already started selling and are looking to do it better. They can certainly get value from this book, but I didn't write it for them. I wrote it for the woman who has nothing but a dream that's stuck inside her mind, trapped by the fear that this business she desperately wants to create can't survive the real world. I'm here to show you that it can do better than survive; with the right beliefs and strategies, you can turn that dream into a thriving business.

If you have a dream, acknowledge it now. Take a minute to give it form. Say it out loud, write it down, draw a picture, make a collage—anything physical to express what you want to achieve as an entrepreneur. Give it a name and set a deadline to accomplish it.

Now, commit to it. The last thing you want is to get all the way through this book and have nothing to show for it— what a waste of time that would be. Better to put it down and watch a movie instead.

No? Ok then, let's make a promise. Not to me, not to yourself, but to your dream. Say to your dream, "I promise to take you seriously and give you the time and attention you deserve. I promise never to stand in the way of your progress. I promise to read this book and take concrete action to bring you to life."

Deal? Let's do this.

CHAPTER 1

FIVE MYTHS OF STARTING A BUSINESS

What do you think of when you hear "salesperson"?

If you're like most people, it's probably nothing good. Maybe it's a scammy cold caller trying to trick you into listening to their pitch. Maybe it's a desperate multilevel marketer pushing products to their family and friends. Better yet, maybe it's that corny guy in the TV commercial telling you to "come on down to Bob's Motors for the best prices in town!"

That's the classic "sleazy salesman" image. In fact, buying a car probably holds the crown of all negative sales stereotypes. Even if you've never done it before, you've heard enough stories to know not to expect a good time. Unfortunately, the stereotype came to life in the worst way when I bought my last car.

I went to the dealership on a Saturday with my husband and our six-month-old daughter. My car had just been totaled, and I needed to replace it ASAP, so I was anxious to drive a new car off the lot that day. I'd done my research and was pretty sure I knew what I wanted. I just needed to get in the car and take it for a spin to be sure. Honestly, it should have been an easy commission for the salesperson and a pleasant experience all around.

Instead, the salesman got off to a bad start immediately. When we walked in, he approached us and addressed my husband, completely ignoring me. Even when my husband emphasized that *I* was buying the car for *me*, this guy didn't get it—he kept talking to both of us instead of focusing on me. When we finally got to the test drive, it only got worse. He seemed impatient as we set up the car seat for our daughter, and had the nerve to look surprised that *I* got in the driver's seat.

Worse, he had no idea what mattered to me and didn't bother to figure it out. He kept going on about things I didn't understand or care about, like engine power and torque. I was a new mom, and what I actually wanted to know was how safe the car was, how many cup holders and window shades it had, and how easy it was to load and clean. But instead of listening to the customer in front of him, our salesman blabbered on about what *he* thought were the car's most important features. By sticking to his script, he imposed *his* values and priorities on me (typical).

From the moment we walked in, I just wanted to get out of there. But I needed a car, and that made me feel like a prisoner, a captive customer with no choice but to put up with this crap. I should have felt excited about my new purchase—a new car that was better than my old one, that had everything I wanted, that I could drive home today! Instead, I felt frustrated, exhausted, and used. This guy got to make a commission off me even though he did nothing to help me. Needless to say, I would never send any of my friends or family there.

That experience was the epitome of what I'll call the *old way* of doing business and sales. It was focused on selling the product, not solving my problem. That made it one-size-fits-all. Even though my husband and I got individual attention, the salesman clearly didn't adjust his approach to fit the people in front of him. The whole thing was transactional—he sold, we bought, and no lasting relationship or loyalty was built.

We've all experienced *The Wolf of Wall Street* selling style at some point, and those vibes dominate the stories we hear about business in movies. But don't be fooled—that's not the only way. I don't run my business like that, and you don't have to either. To be honest, you'll have a much better chance of success if you don't. People only tolerate that type of experience when there's no alternative or the cost of pursuing the alternative is too high. That makes the old way risky because new alternatives can pop up at any time.

The problem is that stereotypes like these persist and skew your idea of what's possible and how you fit into the world of entrepreneurship. They create false ideas of what it means to start and run a business, and those myths can scare you away from pursuing your goals or make it impossible for you to achieve them if you try. They seem innocent enough at first—some even sound like common sense—but these ideas are dream killers.

To be frank, I won't stand for it, and I won't let you either. We're about to bust those dangerous myths so you can clear the path toward the independent, passion-driven life you deserve.

MYTH #1: BUILDING A BUSINESS IS HARDER THAN HAVING A JOB.

Americans idolize startup culture, and the prototypical founder story goes something like this. You start with a genius idea. You quit your job, sacrifice everything, and work 'round the clock until you have proof of concept. You show your proof to investors, who give you oodles of money to make it big. You hire a bunch of young, smart people, and everyone works eighty hours a week to grow the business as fast as possible. A bigger company buys your business for a massive sum or you go public. Either way, you're rich and can finally relax for the rest of your life.

You hear about this online through moguls like Gary Vaynerchuk, and you see it on TV shows like *Shark Tank*, but it's *not* the only way to be an entrepreneur. Actually, it might be the worst way, in my opinion. It leaves you with no time for friends and family, let alone romance. No time to care for others. No time to savor the little joys in life. No time for *you*.

This is one reason why women often get more pushback than men do when they talk about becoming entrepreneurs. When men choose to make those sacrifices to chase their dreams, people usually congratulate them on their courage and dedication. When women do, people often question why they would want to—or whether they can—give up their role as caretaker. *Don't you want a family? Who's gonna take care of your kids while you work?* This attitude is frustrating and can undermine your confidence if you encounter it, but the good news is that starting a business doesn't have to mean sacrificing everything else in your life.

If you have priorities other than making as much money as

possible, you need an alternative model of entrepreneurship, one that allows you to build a business that serves *you*. That story goes something like this. You have a craft or skill that you love and use it to create a product or service that other people value. You offer that for sale and seize every opportunity to refine it so you can attract more people and charge enough to make a good living. You build a strong personal brand that makes it easy to get and keep a healthy client base. Most importantly, you set the boundaries you need to live the way you want.

To me, this method clearly wins over the "go hard, grow fast, cash out" model of Silicon Valley-style startups. Still, you can probably tell that it requires some serious effort, not to mention major courage. So, you might be wondering if it's worth it. Wouldn't it be easier to just have a job?

That depends on what you're prepared to tolerate. Think about risk, for instance. You take risks in building a business, no question. Especially in the beginning, you risk not generating enough revenue to make ends meet or even break even. But it's also risky to depend on someone else's business for your livelihood. A job can disappear overnight on the whim of your boss or some C-suite executive you've never met, and you have no control over it. Plus, you run the risk of having terrible supervisors, coworkers, or clients that you can't get rid of because it's not your choice. You might even suffer from pay discrimination, as so many women do without even realizing it. According to the American Association of University Women, in 2020, women earned eighty-two cents for every dollar earned by men.[1] Among the multiple reasons for this are common employer policies like basing salaries on prior earnings and prohibiting the discussion of wages among employees, which can leave you vulnerable to earning less than your male peers.

Now think about the rewards. A business gives you much more control over your income—as you gain expertise and refine your offerings, you can grow your earnings much faster than any traditional career path would allow. Plus, there's real value in the pride of creating something that's yours and helps others. But you won't get handed traditional corporate benefits like health insurance or a retirement fund, and unless you plan to grow your business to a massive scale, it won't give you the "prestige" of a C-suite title at a Fortune 500 company.

Does a job or a business give you a more balanced life? It depends. Some jobs have reasonable hours and flexible policies, and they let you leave your work in the office at the end of the day. Usually, though, it's not so perfect—the hours are long, the schedule is strict or unpredictable, your boss hounds you after hours, or you can't take time off when you

---

[1] "The Simple Truth about the Gender Pay Gap: 2020 Update," American Association of University Women, accessed July 16, 2021, https://www.aauw.org/app/uploads/2020/12/SimpleTruth_2.1.pdf.

want to. Running a business can take over your life worse than the worst of jobs if you let it, but if you set healthy boundaries and build the infrastructure to keep things running in your absence, it can give you more flexibility than any employer can offer.

Which risks and rewards do you prefer? There's no wrong answer, but if you're thinking that having a business sounds pretty great, we have four more problematic beliefs to tackle.

MYTH #2: MY SKILL/PRODUCT CAN SELL ITSELF.

You're not starting a business to become a salesperson, I know. Except you kind of are.

Hear me out on this—it's not as terrible as it sounds. I coach a lot of women who start businesses around their passion and just want to focus on doing their craft. They're not comfortable with marketing and sales, so they just put their heads down and make their product or service as perfect as it can be. The result might be beautiful, but it's all for nothing if no one shows up to buy it.

People who are proud of their work sometimes suffer from the illusion that the work speaks for itself. Hopefully, that's true to a certain extent. People *should* be able to look at your products or your past work and see quality there. You absolutely do want to impress prospective customers with your gorgeous handmade jewelry, stunning custom websites, or whatever it is you offer. It's true that without that quality, capturing their attention will be tough.

But is that where you want the story to end? Wouldn't it be more powerful if they knew the inspiration behind your designs, why you use certain materials, and how you started making jewelry in the first place? Don't you want them to understand why your websites stand out from the sea of boring templates, helping your clients engage their site visitors longer and convert them into customers more frequently? They won't know if you don't tell them! That, my friend, is marketing and sales.

This is usually where people argue that their past customers can do that through reviews, testimonials, and referrals. Yes, social proof is an important part of a healthy business. You definitely want people to speak highly of their firsthand experience with your work, and that can massively help bring new people in the door. But are you really going to trust someone else to tell your story for you? And if your clients haven't heard it from you first, how will they know what to say?

Bottom line: it's simply not true that the best product always wins. Quality and social proof are essential, but they can't sustain your business by themselves. If you're facing any kind of competition, as most of us are, you need to educate people about why they should choose you over anyone else. And if your competition is sparse, don't get too excited. Marketing is even more important for you because a lack of competition is a sign that your market is either tiny or new. In the first case, you need marketing to grow your potential customer base, and in the second, you need it to explain the value of what you do.

No matter who you are or what your business is, it's part of your job as an entrepreneur to actively tell people that you exist and can solve their problems. This isn't a burden—it's an opportunity. You get to tell the story of your work the way you want and to the audience you want. The alternative is letting other people do that for you, and I can guarantee they won't do it justice the way you can.

MYTH #3: SALES AND MARKETING ARE GROSS.

Sadly, the world still has plenty of salespeople like my friend at the car dealership. Experiences like that make us think that sales and marketing are inherently slimy, manipulative, pushy, impersonal, egotistical, greedy...you get the picture. It's an endemic problem in the sales profession. Sales job ads often use aggressive, masculine language that emphasizes hitting quotas and reaping the financial rewards, so it's no wonder they attract people who will do whatever it takes to close the deal. This approach is why so many people, especially women, believe that any active sales effort is equivalent to hurting the customer or taking something away from them.

Selling your product or service doesn't have to be like that. In fact, it works better if it's not. People love to buy things, but they don't like to be sold to, so it's an advantage *not* to fit the salesperson stereotype. If you approach the process as a collaboration with your customer to solve their problem, you'll connect with them on a personal level and understand their particular needs. They'll feel cared for and heard, and you'll be able to share exactly how your solution will make their life better. The whole process feels great for everyone and makes it much easier for the customer to say yes to your offer and be happy about it.

I want you to think of it like driving a car. The old way of selling puts the salesperson in the driver's seat, and they need to convince the customer to get in and go along for the ride. Is that sketchy or what? The new way—our way—lets the customer do the driving. Your job? Be the navigation system that shows them how to get where they want to go, but they get to be in control of the vehicle. You never have to be pushy or manipulative. All you have to do is understand their goals, ask questions, and provide information to help them get there. When they do, they'll only be grateful.

That's how you turn sales into a win-win proposition. From this perspective, it's no longer something that feels gross and out of step with who you are and what you stand for. Instead, it's a powerful tool for making your life *and* your customers' lives better at the same time. It's an exchange of value that leaves you both happier and builds a genuine human connection.

MYTH #4: I'M NOT DOING THIS TO GET RICH, SO I DON'T NEED TO MASTER MARKETING.

Many women become entrepreneurs because they feel they have something to give. They want to help people, solve problems, and do what they love. Their top motivation isn't money—it's the internal desire to use their own skills and talents to provide something of value to others.

That's great. Having a purpose beyond making money will help you stay focused and motivated even when things get rough, as they always do at some point. But it's a mistake to focus so exclusively on doing what you love that your business becomes unsustainable. You can't afford to neglect marketing because if you don't make enough money to stay afloat and prevent burnout, you'll lose the opportunity to do what you love in the first place.

Imagine Kristi, who has a portrait photography business. She's passionate about her craft but feels weird about selling because making money isn't her primary concern. She started her business so she could do what she loves: taking photos and helping women feel confident. Her mission is to give people photos of themselves that show their inner beauty and individuality, which she knows can raise their self-esteem and help them land a job, get new clients, and even attract their soulmates.

Kristi can run her business in one of two ways. One option is to let her aversion to marketing win and focus exclusively on her mission. She keeps her prices low to make her services accessible to all the people she wants to serve, which includes students and others who struggle to afford the going rate for professional headshots. She gets some clients but never quite enough, and they never seem to fully appreciate all the value she gives them. She has to work a lot to make ends meet, and within a few years, she starts to feel resentment toward her business.

The alternative is to learn to market her work and use that to increase her opportunities to give. In this version, Kristi takes control of her story and proactively reaches out to her audience, targeting people who understand the power of a great photo and want something that will show their true colors and stand out from the pack. She gives away helpful content for free, which provides value to the people who can't afford her services and builds trust with those who can. The result is a steady influx of clients who are thrilled to work with her and pay her premium prices. She earns enough to not have to work constantly, leaving her time to enjoy life and donate her photography services to job seekers at the community employment center.

Which sounds better? Yeah, I thought so.

Selling your services (and being damn good at it) will allow you to do *more* of what you love and make a bigger impact at the end of the day. And remember, you deserve to get paid well for what you do—a balance between feeling financially fulfilled and serving your mission is the key to long-term business success.

MYTH #5: I'M TOO INTROVERTED FOR THIS.

It's easy to think that entrepreneurship is an extrovert's game. It certainly seems like the people shouting about their business success on YouTube and Instagram are an outgoing bunch, right? What you need to realize is that for every entrepreneur who's a natural on camera and thrilled to spend all day talking with strangers, there's another one quietly doing their work and still killing it in their business.

Sales is the lifeblood of any business, so yes, you have to be willing to do the work it takes to make a sale. That means reaching out to people, listening, empathizing, and collaborating with them. How often you have to do this, though, depends a lot on what your business is, so take a moment to imagine it. If you're selling products online, you might not need much face time beyond initial market research and some social media work. If you're offering a custom service, especially something like coaching, you might be talking to people all day, every day.

Think about what the day-to-day reality of your business will look like, including marketing and sales activities. If you're not sure, see if you can find someone with a similar business and talk to them about it. How much time can you expect to spend in the kind of interpersonal situations that drain your energy? Can you arrange it so you get enough rest between these conversations? If the picture that emerges makes you cringe, you're in trouble. Either bow out now, rethink your business idea, or partner with someone you trust who can do that stuff for you.

Remember, though, that it's easier than ever to connect with people while keeping your distance. You can do almost everything online, including creating and sharing content, engaging with your social network, communicating with clients, and even delivering your products or services. You probably can't escape the occasional phone call or meeting, but if you build your business around other modes of communication, you can keep them to a minimum. If you're on the quiet and reserved side, online business can make your life much easier.

Not to mention, there are people out there just like you in

your target audience. Just by standing in your power and owning who you are, you can attract the right type of people your way because they relate to you. Other introverts are out there waiting to feel represented so they can buy from someone like you, and that's the power of a personal brand.

* * *

Does the idea of starting your own business look less foggy with those five myths out of the way? Do you see now why learning to sell the right way should be your top priority if you want to make your dreams come true? It's amazing what a difference it can make to clear out some of the crap our brains soak up from the culture we live in. You *can* do this entrepreneurship thing, and while I can't promise it'll be easy (nothing worth doing ever is), you don't have to sacrifice everything or wait decades to get the results you want.

It all starts with a few basic skills. Like every woman, you already have them and use them every day, just not quite in the way you're about to learn. The raw muscles are there, so let's get cracking on training them to build a business.

CHAPTER 2

OWN YOUR AUTHORITY

The summer after I started my online fitness coaching business, some of my high school friends were home from college, and one evening, we went out to celebrate one of their birthdays. After months with my nose to the grindstone, I was looking forward to a night out, catching up with people I hadn't seen in a while. I was all smiles and hugs when I arrived at the restaurant, ready for good food and good times. But the bottom dropped out of my stomach when someone turned to me and asked one simple question.

"So, Karrie, what have you been up to?"

It sounded innocent enough, and the curiosity was understandable. They were all busy getting college degrees and corporate jobs, so naturally, they wanted to know why I wasn't and what I was doing instead. There was no obvious skepticism or condescension in the air, but even so, the question was a piercing reminder of my inexperience and naivete. I didn't know how to answer the question. Who did I think I was, starting a business at nineteen years old with no clue about anything?

So, bracing myself for judgment, I said, "Oh, I'm just trying to do this thing online...it's basically like personal training, but you know, doing it with more people, um, using social media. Because, you know, I'm taking care of my dad, so I can't get a job...I just kind of want to try my own thing and see how it goes."

You know how an elevator pitch is supposed to quickly convince people to be interested in you or your company? Mine only convinced them to write me off.

"Oh," they responded. "Sounds cool," they said, as supportive friends are supposed to do. Someone else jumped into the awkward silence with a new story, and suddenly I could breathe again.

The conversation with my friends ended there, but it continued internally for me. The words had merged with the undercurrent of self-doubt that constantly circled in the back of my mind and surged up whenever a prospect said no or a meticulously crafted Facebook post got nothing but crickets. Every time someone asked me about my business and I responded with hesitation instead of confidence, I unconsciously fed this mental riptide that dragged me back even when I thought I was swimming forward.

The saddest part is that I kept talking about my business like that for the next two years, thinking I was somehow protecting myself. I was afraid to hear other people diminish my work by questioning the wisdom of my choices or casting doubt on my abilities. Even more, I feared failing and being revealed as a fraud—better to underpromise and overdeliver, right? So, I minimized the seriousness and importance of my efforts, hoping to avoid criticism and escape the scrutiny with my ego intact.

But instead of protecting my fledgling business, I was limiting it. In talking about it as if I were just testing the entrepreneurial waters with a casual side gig, I was teaching everyone around me to treat it that way. In refusing to show how much it meant to me, how much effort I invested in it, and how big my dreams really were, I robbed my business of the chance to be taken seriously.

People responded accordingly. My friends didn't understand why I spent so much time working and often tried to convince me to blow it off. My parents were always supportive, but other family members kept asking when I would go back to school. Worse, my clients never seemed to see me as a legitimate professional, even though I put all my passion, energy, and dedication into my work. I put on a brave face, but they could sense the doubt creeping underneath.

Here's the truth I took *way* too long to understand: if you don't treat your business like a business, no one else will. That applies not just to what you do—the hours, sweat, and money you put in—but also how you talk about it to yourself and *everyone* around you, not just clients. Even if you're just starting out, you have something valuable to offer. Your first priority is to figure out what it is, own it, and make it a little better every day.

MANAGE YOUR SELF-DOUBT

When you start your business, don't be surprised if you feel at least a little bit like you're walking onto the red carpet in a fifty-dollar dress. It's tempting to look around and think everyone else is so much more successful, you don't belong, and any moment someone is going to laugh in your face and throw you out of there.

This feeling that you're a fraud is often called *imposter syndrome*. Psychologists Pauline Rose Clance and Suzanne Imes coined the term in their 1978 study of high-achieving women, which revealed that many of the participants struggled to accept their successes and accolades as genuinely deserved.

Even after years or decades of remarkable achievement, they worried that they weren't really as smart and capable as everyone seemed to believe, and that eventually someone would realize the truth. Since then, a litany of female leaders have publicly spoken about feeling this way, from Facebook COO Sheryl Sandberg to former First Lady Michelle Obama.

While men can and do experience this feeling, it's much more common in women. The reason is simple: women are still relative newcomers to professional work and leadership positions. As Ruchika Tulshyan and Jodi-Ann Burey point out in a 2021 *Harvard Business Review* article,[2] most organizations are still deeply rooted in masculine, white, heteronormative culture. As a result, women and members of other minorities often feel out of place and don't get the kind of affirming feedback that their male, majority-culture counterparts do.

Women typically experience imposter syndrome as a form of constant, low-level anxiety that flares up in situations where they're at a higher risk of being "found out." The feeling can persist even when you're safe and alone because you can't stop worrying about your perceived inadequacy. These emotions can become a major roadblock to your work.[3]

---

2   Ruchika Tulshyan and Jodi-Ann Burey, "Stop Telling Women They Have Imposter Syndrome," *Harvard Business Review*, February 11, 2021, https://hbr.org/2021/02/stop-telling-women-they-have-imposter-syndrome.

3   Danielle Page, "How Imposter Syndrome Is Holding You Back at Work," *Better by Today*, October 26, 2017, https://www.nbcnews.com/better/health/how-impostor-syndrome-holding-you-back-work-ncna814231.

Some women, in an attempt to push past their doubts, fall into burnout-inducing behaviors like perfectionism and overwork. Others shrink back, opting not to speak up, take healthy risks, or pursue their professional ambitions. Either way, imposter syndrome can stall your dreams if you let it.

My entire first attempt at business was basically one long episode of imposter syndrome. As much as I wanted my business to work, I could never stop questioning whether I was capable of achieving my goals. In the beginning, I worried about being too young and inexperienced, and wondered if people saw me as just a kid playing fitness coach. When my clients didn't follow their diet and exercise plans and then quit, I wondered if maybe I wasn't as good at coaching as I thought. When I struggled to make ends meet month after month, I wondered if I was cut out for entrepreneurship at all.

It's normal and healthy to question yourself when you feel at the limits of your abilities or notice something is going wrong. If humans didn't do that instinctively, we probably would be long extinct, having recklessly killed ourselves off by climbing too high and poking too many bears. The problems start when you respond to those questions the way I did: by sinking into self-doubt and staying there.

That's not the only option, which is good, because if you have ambition (which I know you do because you haven't shelved this book yet), you'll never escape the questions. I certainly haven't. Entrepreneurship forces you to grow, and growing means crossing the boundaries of your comfort zone. Every time I do, the questions come up again: *Am I prepared for this? Do I have what it takes? Do I belong here?* I've asked myself those things countless times—when I raised my prices, launched my first online course, got my first feature in *Forbes*. The difference is that now I have the tools and beliefs to respond in a way that drives me forward instead of holding me back.

One of the things that helped me most was the work of Dr. Valerie Young, who has identified five imposter syndrome types based on what kind of unreasonable expectations you set for yourself.[4] The Perfectionist focuses on *how* they do things, and if it's not flawless, it's a failure. The Expert is obsessed with *what* and *how much* they know and are convinced it should be absolutely everything in their field. The Soloist cares about *who* gets the job done, and if it's not you alone, you don't deserve the credit. The Natural Genius concentrates on *how* and *when* they do things, and if it's not fast and effortless, it's not good enough. The Superwoman/Superman is concerned with *how many* roles they can master (professional, wife, parent, hostess, friend, etc.), and they expect to juggle them all perfectly.

---

4   Valerie Young, "The 5 Types of Imposters," ImposterSyndrome.com, accessed July 16, 2021, https://impostorsyndrome.com/5-types-of-impostors.

In the early days of my business, I identified most strongly as The Expert. I thought that even though I was just starting out, I should know everything there was to know about fitness, nutrition, and behavior change, not to mention how to build a business. Dr. Young's framework helped me see how ridiculous that was and gave me the language to call out my unreasonable expectations. When I notice that self-doubt creeping in, I like to write about what I'm thinking and feeling—I'll just jot it down on any convenient scrap of paper, letting the words come out unfiltered. Putting it in writing helps me see whether I'm being realistic or overly hard on myself. If I see that my expectations are out of whack, I can adjust them, which instantly relieves some of the pressure.

So, when you find yourself on that red carpet, thinking you're about to be called out for the fraud that you are, *stop*. Reality check: everyone is doing their own thing and having a good time, and if you just wear that clearance-rack dress like you mean it, you'll fit right in.

SEPARATE YOUR PRICE FROM YOUR WORTH

Let's say you finish reading that last section and decide you're so inspired to reclaim your confidence that you put the book down and get straight to work selling your goods. You're cruising along, congratulating yourself on pushing past your comfort zone, when one word brings you crashing back down into a puddle of doubt: *no*. Maybe all it takes is once;

maybe you hear it dozens of times before it starts to hurt. If you're new to selling your own products or services (which is, of course, why you're here), I can virtually guarantee that at some point, the rejection will sting.

What you're selling is probably tightly linked to who you are or what you've experienced. If it's not a skill you're personally providing or an object your hands made, it's at least your brainchild, and I bet you've invested some serious time in making it awesome. When someone tells you it's not worth the price you're asking, it's hard not to take it personally, especially if you were following the ambiguous advice to "charge your worth."

That saying floats around endlessly in business circles, and it always makes me cringe. Because let's dig into this: how much are you *worth*? You're a human being, and putting a price tag on a person—especially yourself—shouldn't be a thing anywhere, ever. What this little gem of wisdom is *trying* to say is that your price should reflect the value your product or service brings to the customer's life. Your worth as a person has nothing to do with it. The more clearly you can separate your personal worth from your sales, the better off you'll be.

You see, taking rejection personally doesn't just cause unnecessary pain in the moment. It throws a soaking wet blanket over the fire inside you that's generating all the energy to run your business. The instinct to protect yourself is powerful, so if your brain learns that selling presents a potential threat to your personal integrity, it will put up huge barriers to that activity. Instead of approaching sales as an exciting opportunity to put your ideas out into the world and make money, you'll show up full of dread and wishing it were over before it started. Which mindset do you think will result in more people saying yes to your offer? I know I'd be quicker to buy from someone who's obviously psyched about what they're selling—the energy is contagious. When you think about it that way, it's easy to see how confusing sales with your personal worth can spark a vicious cycle of misery and disappointing revenue.

So, how do you stop from slipping down that slope? It's simple. Instead of focusing on yourself, think about the customer.

When someone says no to your offer, all it really means is that your product or service isn't right for them at the price you're charging—which, by the way, is fine! No offer is a perfect fit for everyone. It doesn't mean you have to change what you're doing. You're still you, your work is still amazing, and there are plenty of fish in the sea. Let this one go and cast your line again.

No matter how good you are, sales is always a bit of a numbers game. There's simply no way that your offer is right for everyone, at every point in time—not even for all the people who initially express interest in it. To think that every person you talk to, or even the majority, will be ready to buy from you is just plain unrealistic. Think about your own behavior: how often have you browsed a website or store, watched a webinar, or talked to a salesperson and decided not to buy? Maybe the product wasn't quite what you wanted, your need wasn't strong enough to justify the cost, or it just wasn't the right time to make that purchase. That's a normal part of the shopping experience. I don't know about you, but if I said yes to every sales offer that crossed my path, I would have gone broke a long time ago.

So, don't be surprised if you have to ask lots of times before you get a yes. On web pages, normal conversion rates (that's the percentage of visitors who buy something or take some other valuable action, like signing up for your email list) are around 3 to 6 percent for most industries.[5] Even for inbound phone sales (meaning someone has voluntarily contacted you and is already interested in your offer), only 30 to 50 percent of prospects make a purchase.[6] Marketing is such a huge industry precisely because it takes consistent effort to turn people into customers, and hearing no is a normal part of that process that will never go away.

---

5   "The 2021 Conversion Benchmark Report," Unbounce, accessed July 16, 2021, https://unbounce.com/conversion-benchmark-report.

6   "2015 Call Intelligence Index," Invoca, accessed July 16, 2021, http://go.invoca.com/rs/invoca/images/call-intelligence-index.pdf.

When you feel your emotions spiraling downward over a string of rejections, consider the advice of Jessica Bacal. She literally wrote the book on this subject after interviewing over twenty-five women about the professional rejections and failures that shaped their careers. One common strategy to move past the hurt is to stick to a rigorous work schedule, which forces you to focus your attention on creating rather than on feelings of failure. Another is to envision yourself in the future, reveling in the success you'll enjoy if you keep moving forward despite the rejection. My personal favorite is positive self-talk: remind yourself that it's not you, it's them. Your offer didn't resonate this time, but you still have so much to give to the other people out there who will see the value in it. Plus, remember that a no now doesn't mean no forever. They could come back tomorrow, a week from now, a month from now, and be ready to buy...and at that point, you should still be ready, willing, and excited to sell to them! So, get up and do a little dance to shake off the blues and pump up your energy to keep at it.

BUILD AUTHORITY WITH LIMITED EXPERIENCE

Which came first, the chicken or the egg? Or in the case of your business: your authority or your experience? For many women, solving this puzzle is one of the biggest hurdles in starting a business. If you've never done this before, how on earth will you convince anyone to buy from you, especially if there are other people doing something similar who have clearly been around for a while? And if you can't get customers, how will you ever gain experience?

Fortunately for all of us, there's no universal definition of what an expert is. You don't have to have a PhD in photography to take a dazzling headshot, and you don't have to spend ten thousand hours making jewelry before you create a drool-worthy piece. Unless you're at absolute ground zero, you're always ahead of someone. So, as long as your expertise is at least one step ahead of your customers', you can bring real value to their lives, and they'll gladly pay you good money in exchange.

There's your permission to start. If you were waiting for it, now you have it, courtesy of a certified badass entrepreneur who was in your shoes not that long ago. When I started coaching fitness online, I'd never done any personal training before. All I had was my personal experience in sports and in the gym, plus some basic anatomy knowledge and a certification that anyone with half a brain and three months to study can get. No Olympic athlete would have hit me up for hot workout tips, but I could definitely help the average couch potato take control of their health and start sculpting their body.

Who is your average couch potato, the person who can get real value from the expertise you have right now? It's probably a bigger group than you imagined. Think about a brand-new portrait photographer—let's call her Emma. She's no Annie Leibovitz (yet), but she has a professional camera and knows how to use it. She also knows a little about how to use light, how to style makeup and clothing for the lens, and where to go for a great backdrop. That's waaaay beyond what most people can do, which is to just tap the circle on their smartphone screen and hope for the best. Can she bring real value to someone like that who wants a nice headshot or family portrait? Absolutely. And she doesn't have to pretend to know everything; it's enough to simply know a little more than her clients.

If you want to get anywhere, you have to take the first step, obviously. When you do, give yourself a pat on the back, but don't stop there. How you take the *next* steps determines whether your business accelerates or stumbles along. That's because once you get started, everything you do is an opportunity to learn and get better, but learning doesn't happen automatically. You have to be intentional.

Let's continue with our photographer, Emma. She can cruise along taking photos the way she knows how now, and if she's lucky, she might scratch out a living that way. Her work might even improve a little over time. But she'll find it hard to raise her prices even after she's been at it for a while because no one really cares how long she's been doing this—they care how good the results are, and she hasn't done much to elevate the quality of her work.

Or instead, Emma could invest some of her revenue in an advanced photography class where she can get feedback on her work from someone with more expertise. She could join a group of professional photographers who share their knowledge and critique each other. She could view every client, every shot, as a chance to push her boundaries and do better than last time. Soon, her photos will easily command higher prices, and she'll gain access to clients who are more discerning and willing to pay for a premium product.

It's easy to sit by yourself and not reach for help. In a way, it's ingrained in our culture, part of the American ideal of being self-made. But in my opinion, screw that. You'll get a lot further, a lot faster if you get specific feedback from knowledgeable people whose opinions you can trust—not just your clients, your mom, or your best friend. I've always gotten the best feedback from people who were a couple of steps ahead of me on the same road. I've consulted with other entrepreneurs running similar businesses, experts in fitness, and, later, sales experts.

Education, networking, and collaboration are the gateways to the high-quality feedback you need to build your authority fast. In Chapter 6, you'll learn more about how to build supportive professional relationships. For now, just know that if you surround yourself with people who you aspire to be, you'll always find a leg up to the next level in your business.

DEVELOP YOUR PERSONAL BRAND

No matter how much expertise you have, you'll never be the only person doing what you do. The more internet based your business is, the more truth this holds because your customers can choose from people all over the world. That much is obvious, but here's another thing you might not realize: even if you are the top authority in what you do, that doesn't automatically guarantee an endless flow of customers.

Expertise and quality aren't the most powerful motivators for people to pull out their wallets. If all they wanted was a solution to their problem, an anonymous corporation would do the trick. Luckily for us, most people, especially women, also love to feel emotionally connected to the products and services they buy. They want to know who you are, trust you, and relate to you. Fostering that connection not only attracts your ideal customers but also builds their loyalty so that they come back over and over and recommend you to their friends.

That's the goal of your personal brand. By creating a brand that is uniquely and unmistakably yours, you differentiate yourself from other people who offer something similar. Inevitably, some people will relate better to you over anyone else out there. That's why your authentic voice, perspective, and style are essential to the success of your business.

New entrepreneurs who struggle to define their personal

brand usually end up at one of two extremes: either they sound like a robot or they come off so overly friendly that they seem unserious or overwhelming.

The first problem is a sign that you need to incorporate more stories and personality into everything you do. Even if personal details seem irrelevant to your work, they serve as connection points for customers, signals that you'll understand them better than someone else might. For example, some of the connection points I use are that I'm a woman, I'm a mom, I'm young, and I love dogs. Simple, right? None of these things necessarily makes me a better sales expert, but they do signal to you that I might be the right person to teach *you* how to sell because if you relate to any of those things, you already know I'll understand at least some small aspect of who you are. It's called the Similarity-Attraction Effect—people gravitate toward others who have something important in common with them, especially interests, attitudes, and values.

Take a few minutes now to brainstorm what's different about you. First, let's start with the basics. Where are you from and where do you live now? Do you have a partner, kids, or pets? How would you describe your personality? What are three things you love? Three things you can't stand? How do you like to spend your free time? What do you value most in life?

Now, focus on the skill you're selling and what makes it special. This isn't about how you're better than others but how you're different, so look beyond the deliverables of your work to everything that goes into them. Why do you do what you do? How did you learn to do it? What do you like most about it? What's your approach or perspective? How do you relate to and communicate with your customers? What do you want to help them learn, do, or feel?

Step back and look at all the things that make you unique. If you answered all those questions, it's a lot! All the things you wrote just now are the raw ingredients of your personal brand. You don't have to use *all* of them at once, though. Focus on the elements that mean the most to you, that are the closest to your heart and truly define who you are. Resist the temptation to downplay the personal details—if you let your brand revolve solely around your work, it will be tough to stand out, and you'll miss out on opportunities to connect with people who relate to you and convert them into customers.

You can go out and find entire books just about personal branding, and they can be valuable, but my advice at this stage is to keep it simple. Don't let "developing your personal brand" become an excuse for not moving forward and actually selling things. Brands always evolve over time, and when you're raking in the dough, I have no doubt you'll want to spend more time refining your brand. I sure did, and more than once.

For now, though, all you need to do is pick the key elements of *you* that you want to highlight in your business and use them *everywhere*. Your brand should be crystal clear and consistent on your website, social media, emails, ads, storefront, product packaging, business cards, and any other place where your business exists, on the web or in the physical world. If you have other people working with you or creating things for you, they need to understand your brand and commit to representing it. Anytime someone comes into contact with your business, their experience should reflect who you are and what you stand for. That doesn't just include customers. It also applies to vendors, business partners, employees, media representatives, and the general public. If you craft your brand thoughtfully and use it consistently, over time, it will become your greatest asset.

Like I said at the beginning of this chapter, the definition of *expert* is squishy at best. Who you consider an expert in a given skill or field depends on how much you already know about it and how much knowledge you need to get where you want to go with it. A kid who wants to learn how to swim in their neighborhood pool doesn't need lessons from Michael Phelps, and a woman who wants a cute dress for her next date doesn't need an Armani ball gown. Both of those people would be better served by someone who is much closer to them on the spectrum of expertise.

So, wherever you are on that spectrum right now, even if it's just one notch above total noob, you can be of service to someone else, and you are perfectly justified in asking for monetary compensation for the value you provide. Your expertise can grow over time, and with it your authority and revenue, but not if you never start. The first few steps are the hardest, but if you deliberately use them to study the terrain and improve your form, you'll pick up speed quickly.

Looking back at my first attempts to build a business, it's painfully obvious to me that I didn't fail because I was too inexperienced—I failed because I didn't own the experience I had. As a result, I spent two years treading water, investing a huge amount of time and energy into going absolutely nowhere. There's no reason for it other than my own fear and self-doubt, and when I finally cast those unhelpful thoughts aside, my business gained momentum faster than I ever imagined.

This chapter has been all about you, but you're only half the picture in your business—your customer is the other half. Next, you'll learn to leverage your natural skills to connect with and understand her.

CHAPTER 3

HARNESS YOUR EMOTIONAL INTELLIGENCE

Remember what happened when I bought my last car? Don't worry, I won't rehash that story. (I'd rather not think about it ever again, to be honest.) I only bring it up so you can compare it to my experience buying a house. If that car dealership represented everything we all hate about sales, my realtor was everything you're about to learn to *love*.

Back in early 2020, my husband and I were living in a rented house in Los Angeles. The location wasn't great, the space wasn't ideal, and we had one persistent and moderately terrifying problem: our dog kept jumping the low front fence and running into the street. Every time it happened, as soon as he was safe inside and my heart stopped trying to pound a hole through my chest, I thought we *had* to find a new place.

So when Covid-19 hit and the resulting economic crisis sent interest rates to rock-bottom, we decided it was a sign from the universe that we should buy a house. As far as purchasing decisions, it hardly gets bigger or scarier than that for most people. It's a huge financial commitment, not to mention you have to live every single day with your choice, possibly for decades, so there's a lot riding on making a good decision. A bad one could leave you stuck with nightmares like endless repairs, expensive renovations, unpleasant neighbors, constant security worries, or worse. Plus, the legal processes involved are a complete mystery, especially for first-time buyers like us, and I knew that my self-employed status would complicate the mortgage application substantially.

For all those reasons, I was determined to find a realtor I could trust to protect our interests and find the perfect house for our family. So, I reached out to a friend, who connected me with a realtor she knew personally and recommended highly. It was the right move. In our very first conversation, everything we talked about revolved around what my husband and I wanted. She started by asking about our nonnegotiables, what we absolutely couldn't live without in our new house and neighborhood. Then we talked about other features we'd love to have and the architectural styles that appealed to us. From the way she listened to us, asked insightful questions, and addressed our concerns about the process, we immediately felt understood and taken care of.

Over the few weeks as we arranged the financing and looked at houses, our realtor repeatedly showed that she understood our need for quick communication and always kept in mind what we were looking for. And considering that the number of houses for sale was way below normal levels because of the pandemic, we had a remarkably easy time finding our dream house. We toured about ten houses over the span of three weeks, put in offers on two, and ended up with exactly what we wanted.

"You're so emotional," is a criticism women hear all too often, but it's actually our superpower. Remember that women have a stronger drive than men to connect emotionally with other people, and it has both biological and social roots. We've evolved for *and* been trained all our lives to connect emotionally. That ability to read, feel, and influence emotions is an asset with real economic value. It's what our realtor used to win our trust, find a house we wanted to buy, and of course, take home the five-figure commission she rightfully earned for arranging the deal. Soon, it'll be what *you* use to attract customers who are thrilled to work with you and pay you well for the value you add to their lives.

THE OLD WAY AND THE NEW WAY

The art of sales is undergoing a transformation, and we're all living in a messy, in-between moment when the old way and the new way of doing things coexist. In a way, that's helpful for you because in comparing the two, the one thing that sets them apart becomes impossible to ignore: emotional intelligence.

The standard definition says that emotional intelligence is the ability to perceive and influence emotions, both other people's and your own. When it's missing, salespeople tend to do whatever it takes to secure their desired outcome. That includes reaching out blindly to prospects, often using mass cold calls and other aggressive, impersonal tactics. They ignore or push past objections, sticking to a script that focuses on what they view as the important selling points of their offer. If you watch this type of salesperson at work, they spend most of their time talking or expressing themselves, which is what men are typically socialized to do from their earliest days. Essentially, they try to talk the other person into saying yes.

The new way, in contrast, puts emotional intelligence at the center of everything that happens in the sales process. As a seller, your primary aim is to understand the customer's needs or problems, and you do that by listening—not just to respond, but to understand. You get out of your own head and into the customer's by paying attention not only to what they're saying, but also how they're saying it, and what they're *not* saying. Your focus, instead of being on expressing yourself, is on serving the other person, which is what women are socialized to do. This emotionally informed sales process works better and feels better for everyone.

In my early business days, I sold the way I thought I was supposed to, modeling my tactics on what I saw around me and the people that dominated the entrepreneurship airwaves (mostly men). Although I was a woman selling to mostly women, I was using old-fashioned masculine tactics without even realizing it. The result was that I talked too much, neglected to listen, and never primed prospects enough, so they weren't ready to buy from me when I pitched them.

Let me show you exactly what I mean. The following comparison details each step of the sales process, the old way and the new way side by side.

THE OLD WAY	THE NEW WAY
1. Make a cold pitch	*1. Attract through content*
Reach out to people who have no relationship with you or your company yet and interrupt their lives without permission when they're not seeking to interact with you.	Publish helpful articles, videos, podcasts, and social media posts for your target audience. Raise their awareness of the problem they need to solve and the solution you're offering. Provide real value to your prospects through free educational content before they become customers.
2. Tease value or stoke fear	*2. Help them know, like, and trust you*
Give tantalizing hints of the benefits they'll experience if they buy from you. Make them curious, but don't give away too much or their curiosity will be satisfied and they'll have no motivation to buy. Alternatively, harp on pain points to make them fear that if they don't buy, their problem will get even worse.	Build their trust in your expertise and their emotional connection with your brand by helping them get micro wins, make educated decisions, and connect with your personal experience and understanding of the industry.
3. Standard sales pitch	*3. Customize the sales process*
Regardless of who the prospect is, the offer is the same, so deliver it the same way. Talk about the broad features and benefits that make the offer attractive in general and that you think they care about.	Recognize that different customers have different needs and priorities, and during any sales conversation, adjust your explanation of the offer to address their concerns and emphasize what matters most to the particular person (or group of people) you're talking to.

LISTEN WITH EMPATHY

Empathy, which is the ability to feel what someone else is feeling, is a crucial piece of emotional intelligence. It's different from sympathy, which is a sense of pity for someone or agreement with their views. In contrast, empathy involves not only reading someone else's emotions but also sharing them.[7]

---

7   Karsten Stueber, "Empathy," *The Stanford Encyclopedia of Philosophy* (Fall 2019), ed. Edward N. Zaltz, last modified June 27, 2019, https://stanford.library.sydney.edu.au/entries/empathy.

It's a crucial part of how people understand and connect to each other, since we can't actually read each other's minds. Scientists have even observed empathy at a neurological level. Brain imaging studies show that when we observe other people's actions, our brain activity tends to mimic theirs.

According to Frances Frei and Anne Morriss, experts on trust in the business world, empathy is one of three foundational elements of building trust with your customers.[8] The others are logic (customers' belief that you can do what you're saying) and authenticity (their belief that they're interacting with the real you); we tackled both of those in Chapter 2. You can think of these three factors as the legs of a stool, and your customers' trust in your business sits right on top. If one leg is weak, the whole thing could topple over. To build and maintain your customers' trust, it's essential that your customers see that you genuinely care about them.

As a woman, you already have an advantage here. Research shows that women tend to demonstrate greater empathy than men, although the magnitude of this difference depends on the cultural context.[9] This suggests that women's "empathy advantage" is the result of nature *and* nurture. As the primary caretakers of children, women have likely evolved

---

8 Frances X. Frei and Anne Morriss, "Begin with Trust," *Harvard Business Review*, May–June 2020, https://hbr.org/2020/05/begin-with-trust.

9 Claudia Strauss, "Is Empathy Gendered and, If So, Why? An Approach from Feminist Psychological Anthropology," *Ethos* 32, no. 4 (December 2004): 432–457, https://doi.org/10.1525/eth.2004.32.4.432.

to have greater sensitivity to the emotions of others, including infants who can't express their needs in words. Then, when children begin forming their gender identities, girls adopt the traits they observe in their mothers, while boys move away from them. Girls' tendency toward conversation-focused play further develops their empathy, and as they grow up, cultural role models reinforce it. Power structures can play a role too, since people in subordinate positions tend to be more attuned to the emotions of others, and far more women than men find themselves in those roles. Whether any of this is how a just and equal society *should* be is questionable, but it's the reality of our culture today.

So as a woman, you naturally have a high capacity for empathy. That's the good news. The bad news is that modern life can undermine that skill, directing our attention in a million directions except toward the person in front of us. According to one study, empathy among college students has dropped by 40 percent in the last three decades,[10] probably because of how technology has changed the way we communicate.

Thankfully, the damage isn't inevitable or permanent. Intentional practice can strengthen your empathy and keep it top of mind. You can incorporate a few practices into your everyday life to amplify your empathy:

---

10 Sara H. Konrath, Edward H. O'Brien, and Courtney Hsing, "Changes in Dispositional Empathy in American College Students Over Time: A Meta-Analysis," *Personality and Social Psychology Review* 15, no. 2 (August 5, 2010): 180–98, https://doi.org/10.1177/1088868310377395.

Talk to new people. Invite a casual acquaintance out to lunch to get to know them better or strike up a conversation with that neighbor you always wave to but have never actually met. Even better, join a group oriented around a shared goal, like a community garden, political activism committee, or hey, even a business group. Organizations like these tend to bring together people from different backgrounds, which makes them great for exposing yourself to new perspectives.

Practice curiosity. In every conversation, make curiosity your highest priority. Go beyond the usual small talk with deeper questions that provoke more intimate, genuine dialogue. Follow that up with great listening. Especially if you're usually the one to dominate the airwaves, stay quiet and focus on taking in what the other person is sharing.

Try out a different life. Get out of your comfort zone and try on a new outlook by doing things outside your normal routine, which can open your mind to the ways other people's lives and views are different from yours. Start by traveling to a new place or even just visiting a new neighborhood in your city. Do something you've never done before, like playing a new sport, learning a new skill, or going to an event that isn't up your usual alley. Read books about people who are unlike you, whether it's a biography or fiction.

If you do a few of these things every day, you'll quickly notice your instinct for empathy becoming stronger. Still, if sales situations make you nervous or uncomfortable, it can put you in your own head and block that instinct. To get unstuck, it helps to ask yourself questions that shift your focus to the other person. For example, are you hearing what they're saying? How are they saying it? What are they not saying? Reminders like these will prompt you to refocus your attention on the other person so your natural empathy can go to work.

READ THE ROOM

Empathy—perceiving and sharing other people's emotions—is just one piece of the emotional intelligence you'll need to master sales. Another is managing those emotions. That's the skill that will allow you to lead them from wherever they are when they come in contact with you (or your brand), to where they need to be to happily buy from you.

Just imagine my fitness coaching business for a moment. My ideal customer was a woman who wanted to take control of her health and her body image but couldn't do it alone. Before she found me on Instagram, she was feeling pretty crappy about her body. She probably experienced anxiety about her health, confusion about what to eat and how to exercise, and shame for not living up to her aspirations in these areas.

That is *not* the headspace of someone who's ready to shell

out serious money for high-end fitness coaching and dive into the program with unstoppable enthusiasm. To be ready to buy, she needed to feel convinced that her problem was solvable, excited that I had the right solution for her, and confident that with my help, she would be capable of producing the results she wanted. My job was to lead her down that path from anxiety and self-doubt to trust and self-empowerment. Every touch point she experienced, from my social media posts to my website to a one-on-one sales call with me, contributed to that transformation.

We'll talk more about using your published content to influence your audience's emotions in the next chapter. Here, let's focus on what happens in a personal interaction with a prospect because in these situations, you're talking to an individual person, so you need to adjust for their particular personality and values. This is the skill of reading the room: managing the sales environment to keep it optimal for the specific person you're dealing with.

If you're thinking this doesn't apply to you because you run an e-commerce shop and customers buy without talking to anyone, don't skip this section. No matter what kind of business you run, these one-on-one conversations will come up in one form or another. It could be a customer service call where you have to solve a problem someone is having with your product. It could be a conversation with a vendor where you have to convince them to prioritize your order.

It could be an interview with a shop that's interested in carrying your goods. Opportunities to influence people come up all the time, and if you pay attention now, you'll have a better chance of swaying them in your favor when you get the chance. (For simplicity, I'll talk about conversations with prospective customers, but you can generalize the concepts to other types of interactions.)

While every person is unique, there are certain common tendencies that emerge in buyer-seller interactions. Thank goodness, because otherwise you'd have to craft a communication strategy from scratch every time you start a conversation. There's no need for that if you learn how to identify and respond to the four most common types of buyers.

The following categorization is based on the DISC method of personality analysis, which is widely used in marketing and dates back to research by William Moulton Marston in the 1930s. But that framework can get complex and confusing, so I've adapted it specifically for the context of sales using the language I've found most helpful for me and the women I've coached.

BUYER TYPE 1: BOTTOM LINE

This person wants to get straight to the punchline, a.k.a. what they're going to get out of your offer. That includes both literally what they'll receive from you (e.g., weekly coaching calls and a custom nutrition and workout plan) *and* the benefit they'll get out of it (e.g., accountability, freedom from decision-making around food and exercise). They know what they're looking for and often have a deadline for making a decision, even if it's self-imposed. They are competitive, dominant, and like to position themselves as a leader.

To keep a Bottom Line customer happy, you've got to be efficient and get to the heart of the pitch right away. Don't spend a lot of time chatting about other subjects or building up to it. Ask enough questions to get a good understanding of their particular needs and get right to explaining how your product or service can fulfill them. Many times, you can use their competitive nature to your advantage. This type of person values being and having the best, so if you position your premium offering as something that can set them apart and provide the highest-quality outcome, they're likely to find that attractive.

BUYER TYPE 2: PERSONAL CONNECTION

This type of customer values relationships above all else. Their primary goal in the sales process is to be understood, accepted, and deeply involved. They're unlikely to make decisions quickly because they need to get to know you first, and if you don't let them, they probably won't buy. They want to see that you're empathetic and trustworthy, so they ask lots of questions (sometimes personal ones) and listen to you intensely. Because they want that emotional connection, their vibe tends to be laid back, informal, and friendly.

Match that atmosphere and take the time to build rapport— you won't get anywhere if you try to skip or rush this process. Your content should do some of this work for you (as it should for all customers, but it's especially crucial for this type of person). Don't be surprised if they casually engage with your content and chat with you on social media for months before buying. In a sales conversation, help them feel comfortable trusting you with their problem by sharing stories of other happy customers who have benefited from buying from you. If they see that you've helped other people and maintained good relationships with them, they'll be much more inclined to believe you can solve their problem too.

BUYER TYPE 3: GUT FEELING

This type of person has a strong personality, lots of energy, and relies heavily on intuition for making decisions. They're confident in themselves and can move quickly from one idea or point to the next. To get to yes, they need to get that gut feeling that buying from you will make them better off on a human level in the long run. For that reason, they care a lot about the ongoing relationship with you after the initial purchase.

With these people, don't spend too much time on facts, figures, and details that will slow their roll. Instead, focus on the meaningful benefits. Throughout the conversation, check in to ensure you're on the same page by giving them opportunities to confirm that everything you're saying is making sense to them. Also, be sure to highlight how you'll support them after they buy to help them get the benefit they want from your product or service. Let them know that your customer service process won't leave them abandoned after they've made their payment and received the goods.

BUYER TYPE 4: ANALYSIS

The primary goal of this type of person is to minimize risk, so they analyze everything. They want to know all the facts and figures and will ask lots of detailed questions in an effort to be 99.9 percent sure of their decision to buy or not. Not only do they want to fully vet you, but they also want to understand all the other options for solving their problem. That means they tend to take the longest out of the four buyer types to make a decision.

There's no shortcut when it comes to selling to this type of customer, so don't try to push them to make up their mind faster than they want to. The best way to keep things moving along is to provide as much information as possible up front and answer all their questions clearly so they can see that you have nothing to hide and want to help them make the best decision for them. Avoid using flowery, abstract language or making claims that you can't back up with data because this can make them lose confidence in your knowledge and become skeptical of your expertise. The best strategy is to lay out the key features and benefits of your offer in a no-frills, factual manner, which will help them feel empowered to make an informed choice.

From now on, every time you talk to a customer, challenge yourself to identify their buyer type. Keep it simple—a given person might show behaviors associated with multiple buyer types, but one will always be stronger than the others. That's the one that matters and will give you the best chance of managing the room successfully and leading them to a state of mind where they're ready to say yes to your offer.

Now that you get the gist of the four buyer types, take a minute to figure out which one you are. Go with your gut—which of these descriptions resonated with you the most when you first read it? When was the last time you made a nonroutine purchase, and how did you decide what to buy? What kind of information did you look for, and what feelings did you experience that made you decide to go for it? It's helpful to know your own buyer type because we all tend to sell to others in the way we'd like to be sold to. Being aware of this will make you less likely to project your buyer type onto others and more likely to adapt the sales conversation to their needs and desires.

MANAGE YOUR EMOTIONS

The last emotional intelligence skill you need to cultivate is your ability to manage your own emotions. There are two important steps involved: disconnecting your ego from the result of the sale and meeting the customer where they are.

The first step has close ties to what you learned in the previous chapter about separating your price from your self-worth. If you're emotionally hung up on whether you'll get a yes or a no, there's no way you'll be able to listen with empathy and adapt your response according to the customer's needs and personality. You'll end up interpreting every objection, question, or refusal as a personal attack, and that can leave you feeling nervous, angry, or dejected. With those emotions in the room, you'd be amazed at how quickly the sales process can unravel.

There's an easy perspective shift that solves this problem immediately: the sale isn't about *you* at all—it's about the customer. If you're thinking too much about yourself, you'll get stuck in your head when you really need to be in *their* head. They need you to help them solve a problem, so the more you focus on listening to them and showing them how your solution will improve their problem, the easier it will be to take your ego out of the equation.

I'm not a mindset coach, but for my students who have trouble managing their emotions during sales conversations, I do recommend using practices like affirmations, mantras, and meditation to get in the right mindset before a sales conversation. Remind yourself that you are more than this one sales conversation, that sales is a numbers game, and that you're about to get the chance not only to help someone but also make money and advance your skills. During the conversation, check in with yourself occasionally and ask who you're paying attention to, yourself or the other person. If you apply these simple practices regularly, pretty soon you'll approach every sales conversation with excitement and a sense of possibility.

Once your ego is in check, you need to meet your customer where they are emotionally. Mismatched vibes are uncomfortable. Just imagine, if you were a customer concerned about a serious problem and the salesperson was overflowing with optimism and cheer, would you feel that she understood your situation? If you were a woman on a mission ready to get the job done and the salesperson was the definition of zen, would you think she was the right person to help you?

This is similar to what you learned in the previous section, but instead of adapting your sales strategy to fit the customer's values, you'll adapt your energy to fit theirs. We do this all the time without thinking about it. We smile when other people smile, laugh when they laugh, cry when they cry. When we're face-to-face, we even copy each other's gestures and facial expressions unconsciously. It's called mirroring, and the more it happens in a conversation, the more each person feels they're on the same wavelength as the other.

That's what you want your customers to feel when they talk to you. So, mirror their emotional state and energy level at the start of the sales conversation. Whatever they're feeling about the problem they need you to solve—concern, enthusiasm, curiosity, frustration, or something else—show that you understand and empathize with their emotions around this issue. This will make them much more open to following your lead as you guide them toward the emotional state you *want* them to be in. Of course, if someone comes to you frustrated, the idea isn't that you mirror that and spend the entire conversation feeding each other's annoyance. Instead, get on the same wavelength by showing that you *get* their frustration, then lead them toward relief by explaining how you can solve their irritating problem.

✳ ✳ ✳

After reading this chapter, your emotional intelligence systems should be on high alert. If you pay close attention to this crucial skillset, you can strengthen it just by going about your daily life. No need to set aside time to practice, meditate, or reflect on it. Just keep doing what you do—working, studying, shopping, playing, socializing, caring for others—but with a more conscious awareness of the emotions in and around you. Who's feeling what? How can you tell? How can you make them feel better and strengthen their connection with you?

Cultivating your emotional intelligence is good for all your relationships, but pay special attention to how it affects business interactions. As a customer, when have you felt thrilled about a purchase? Frustrated or underwhelmed? In each of those circumstances, what was your relationship with the seller or brand? Now, whenever you buy something, notice those feelings and try to identify where they come from. This deliberate practice and heightened awareness will strengthen your emotional intelligence, and soon you'll feel like you can almost read your customers' minds.

CHAPTER 4

PERSUADE WITH DESIRE AND PAIN

Fitness is a crowded market, and when I first got into it, I knew I'd be competing with plenty of other online coaches, not to mention gyms, boot camps, diet programs, and every other possible pathway to getting physically fit. Unfortunately, just because I was aware of the competition didn't mean I had the slightest clue how to compete effectively.

My communication strategy was a confused medley of vanity, hype, and "exciting" special offers (as my Facebook Memories keep reminding me). I put massive effort into sculpting my body and then showed it off on social media with captions like, "A lot of you have commented on my photos saying you wish you could look like me—WELL, YOU CAN! Let me help you get there! 💪🏋" Every post was overloaded with vague information, capital letters, and exclamation points, like this gem: "If anyone wants to change their life and get healthier, TODAY IS THE DAY! Send me an email and let's get started!!"

When that didn't do the trick—and it never did—I resorted to steep discounts like this one: "I currently have a twelve-week training program on sale for $230, that's a little over $75 a month which is a crazy deal! Email me for more info!"

Yikes. I was like a walking Hallmark card crossed with a bad infomercial, and no one was buying. If you wanted to know what set me apart from other coaches, my content would have left you scratching your head...and looking for the next option.

When I learned to craft my messaging the smart way, everything changed. I started leading with value-driven content—tidbits of helpful information to get people to trust me. I stopped playing the hero of the story (look at *my* healthy and delicious breakfast!) and put the reader in that position instead (*you* can make a healthy and delicious breakfast like this one!). I crafted different hooks to draw people in depending on the specific problem they faced, like emotional eating or feeling overwhelmed at the gym.

All I did was change my words, and suddenly I went from being lost in a sea of fitness options to magnetically attracting exactly the type of client I wanted to train. Even in this hypersaturated industry, the right communication strategy had the power to turn my failing business around completely.

That strategy was based on one simple principle: people buy to fulfill desires and alleviate pain. Every time someone makes a purchase, their goal is to feel better, and they believe the thing they're buying will do the trick. Specific desires and pain points are like radio frequencies—if you can dial into the ones your audience is already listening to, you can connect with them and draw them to you.

IDENTIFY DECISION DRIVERS

If you ask consumers to explain why they bought a certain product or service, they'll often point to measurable factors like price, performance, convenience, or distinguishing features. They're not wrong, but studies by marketing psychologists have found that these superficial factors matter a lot less than you—or the consumer—would expect. The purchasing choices people make reveal that we all routinely rank "logic" below a much more powerful force: emotions.

Marketing and psychology research have shown over and over that emotions play a bigger role than any other factor in purchasing decisions and brand loyalty.[11] Scientists have

---

11 Peter Noel Murray, "How Emotions Influence What We Buy," *Psychology Today*, February 26, 2013, https://www.psychologytoday.com/us/blog/inside-the-consumer-mind/201302/how-emotions-influence-what-we-buy.

even seen this in brain imaging, which shows that brain areas involved in emotion are more active than logic areas when people are evaluating brands. Modern companies repeatedly find that when they redesign their offerings and marketing to be emotion-driven, the result is remarkable growth.[12]

To sell effectively, you need to understand the specific emotions that are driving your target customers and connect them to the results you provide. This is what allows customers to feel emotionally connected with your brand and choose you over all the other options out there. If you make this connection strong enough, they'll buy from you happily without thinking twice, then tell all their friends about you and come back for more...and that's exactly what you're hoping for.

Selling this way isn't just more effective for you. It's also helpful for your customers because the fact is, it's really hard to weigh the facts about all the alternatives for any given purchase. Even for something as simple as a pillow, the task is daunting. There are at least a dozen options at every home goods store, not to mention thousands more online. Each one has a particular brand, size, material, shape, and price. All you want is a good night's sleep. How can you know which one is best for you if the pillow makers don't help you out?

---

12   Scott Magids, Alan Zorfas, and Daniel Leemon, "The New Science of Customer Emotions," *Harvard Business Review*, November 2015, https://hbr.org/2015/11/the-new-science-of-customer-emotions.

Your customers' true emotional drivers can be different from what they initially say. To get at the gold, you have to dig past the surface. For example, Megan, a bride-to-be who is looking for a wedding photographer, might say that her desire is to have beautiful wedding photos. Well, she and every other bride in the world, right? But if she keeps talking, Megan might say that she wants to capture what's special about her relationship with her fiancé in that moment of happiness so that she can be reminded of it every day. Maybe her fiancé hates being in photos, and she's worried all the shots of him will come out with stony faces or fake smiles. Maybe she's already looking forward to changing her profile picture to the envy-inducing shot of glowing love in a perfect white dress.

There's a whole world of specific aspirations, intentions, worries, and frustrations swirling around in your customers' heads before they've ever even heard of you. The magic happens when you anticipate them and talk about them in your messaging. Then, when they come in contact with you, the first thing they see makes them think, *She's reading my mind!* Just imagine if Megan was researching wedding photographers and found an article called "How to Get Gorgeous, Natural Smiles in Every Wedding Shot." Would she click through? You bet she would, and she'd land on the website of a photographer who understands her clients' emotional drivers.

Notice what I did there with that article headline. The customer's fear of having stilted smiles in her wedding photos is a pain point, but the article isn't about having the pain—it's about alleviating it. Pain is a very real driver of many buying decisions, but you never want your messaging to solely focus on the negative. Instead, you want to acknowledge it and focus on how to eliminate it or achieve the opposite state.

DO YOUR MARKET RESEARCH

The process of crafting your message starts with market research. That's a catchall business term for any activity that sheds light on who you're selling to and how to do a better job, and it can include anything from casual conversations with customers to sophisticated industry reports. Don't worry, you don't have to mess with those yet, but you do need to collect some intel on your target audience. Playing guessing games or going off your own personal experience will only get you so far. The sooner you start talking to actual prospects and customers, the better.

First, you've got to decide who you want to serve. If your answer is "everyone," let me kindly but firmly say that you are wrong. Nothing is for everyone. There's no product or service on this planet that everyone wants. Just look at drinking water—we all need it, but there are about 5,742 different brands of it available, not to mention free tap water. Just because your products or services could in theory benefit anyone who chose to use it, not everyone is really going to make that choice, and some will get more out of it than others. *Nothing is for everyone.*

Glad we got that cleared up. So now, who *does* your business serve? The key here is to be as specific as possible. There's a massive temptation to stay broad and say you serve "women" or "people seeking personal growth" or "pet lovers." The problem is that each of those categories includes billions of people with an endless variety of emotional drivers. You could never hope to even come close to understanding all of them, let alone addressing them in your messaging. Even if you did, your messaging would be either so confusing or so general that it doesn't connect with *anyone*. If you aim for everyone, you'll reach no one.

What's the opposite of aiming for everyone? Aiming for one person! This is your ideal customer, and she can be a real person, a blend of multiple people, or a fantasy built from scratch. I know what you're thinking. *If I craft my message around one person, won't I be excluding people from my business and leaving money on the table unnecessarily?* Actually, no. Even a hyperfocused message will still attract a diverse array of people who share the emotional drivers of your ideal customer.

So, let's narrow the field. Who did you have in mind when you created your business? Who do you identify and connect with most? Who has the greatest need for your solution?

Who gets the most benefit out of it or appreciates it the most? When you close your eyes and imagine the *perfect* customer, who do you see? Keep this person in mind—we'll be coming back to her in a minute.

The next step is to check out the competition. What brands or people are doing what you want to do, at the level you want to do it? For example, when I relaunched my fitness coaching business, I wanted to build an audience that was big enough to produce a multiple six-figure income while still allowing me to manage the business mostly on my own. So, I didn't look at massive fitness empires like Beachbody or Jillian Michaels. Instead, I looked to individual fitness influencers on social media who offered the type of service I wanted to provide.

I like to think of this process not as researching the competition so much as discovering and tracking your idols. Find the brands you can look to as role models and study what makes them successful. Who is their target audience? What kinds of products and services do they offer? What marketing strategies do they use? How do people respond to them in reviews and social media? What could you do even better? The point isn't to become a copycat. Your goal here is just to get a sense for who else is out there in your market and what works well—or doesn't—for them. This helps you understand what steps might help you achieve your goals as well as how to stand out from the pack.

Now, it's time to start talking to people. Remember your ideal customer? Find at least five people like her who are willing to talk to you one-on-one for fifteen minutes. If you already have some existing customers or followers who resemble your ideal client, start with them. If not, look to your family, friends, and friends-of-friends. If that doesn't get you what you need, go to where your ideal customer spends time, online or in the real world. Strike up conversations and tell people you're starting a business for people just like them and their input would be hugely valuable in helping you serve them better. Everyone wants to be heard, especially when it comes to the problems that matter to them. You would be surprised by how many people are willing to donate a few minutes to a stranger for the chance to shape something that's intended for them.

If you feel awkward asking for someone's time and input, that's completely normal. One thing that can help you feel more confident is to offer something to show your gratitude. Buy them a coffee, give them a small gift card, or offer a free sample of your product or service. It doesn't have to be super valuable—just a little something to show your appreciation.

The goal of the conversation is to understand where they are now, where they want to go, and how your product or service can help them get from A to B. As they talk, pay close attention to the specific words they're using and the emotions they're expressing. You'll need to use both in your messaging, so it's a good idea to record the conversation (always ask permission first) or at least take notes. Below are some good questions to ask. Feel free to adjust them for your particular circumstances, and follow up each question by asking *why*.

- Regarding this issue, what does your life look like right now? What are you currently doing to solve the problem, and how is it working for you?
- What are your goals? If an ideal solution existed, what would it look like?
- What are you searching for, and what do you value when it comes to purchasing a solution?

To give you an example of how a conversation like this might go, let's say Alexis is a sustainable jewelry designer, and her ideal customer is a young woman who loves to accessorize, pays attention to fashion trends, and wants to feel cute and put-together. She doesn't have a lot to spend, and she prefers to give her hard-earned dollars to companies that are good stewards of the planet and of humanity.

So, Alexis interviews a college student who fits the profile. The interviewee says that she likes to look good when she goes to class because she thinks that not putting effort into her appearance makes her feel lazy and unserious. She knows that first impressions matter, and she wants to make a good one not only on her professors but also her classmates, who could become collaborators, friends, or even romantic partners. She's on a tight budget and can't afford to buy the designer clothes she'd love to have, so she uses jewelry to dress up her outfits. She hates to spend money on things that fall apart or go out of style quickly, and she loves pieces that not only look unique but have an interesting story she can share if someone asks about them. She believes she can make a positive impact on the world through her buying decisions, so she's a vegetarian and tries to find sustainable alternatives to products she knows are damaging to the environment, like single-use plastics. She has looked for eco-friendly jewelry before, but the good-looking brands were too expensive, and the affordable ones looked cheap.

Do you see how this short conversation is a gold mine for messaging? This one person has revealed multiple emotional drivers, key words, and ways in which the existing options in this market are failing to fulfill her needs. Five conversations like this one will give you more than enough to start crafting a message that your ideal customer will find impossible to ignore.

Have fun with your market research because once you start, you're never really going to stop. Every bit of feedback on your business can be valuable, especially if it comes from your ideal customer, so ask for it whenever you can. Invite customers to tell you what they think when they make a purchase (or decide not to), interact with customer support, or engage with your content. Ask them to tell you about their desires and pain points, what they like and don't like about your offer, and how you can serve them better.

Then, listen to what they say and use it! Of course, you don't have to cater to every whim, and you'll never be able to please everyone. Feel free to ignore feedback that doesn't align with your vision or comes from someone who isn't your ideal customer. But if you evolve and improve your offerings to better fit the people you *want* to serve, only good things can come of it.

DESIGN YOUR MESSAGING PILLARS

Once you understand who you're talking to and the specific emotions and goals that drive them, it's time to start publishing content. At a minimum, that includes your website, emails, and social media posts. It can also include blog posts, videos, podcasts, downloadable resources, articles in other publications, or any other way of getting your ideas out in public. You don't have to do all of these, but I highly recommend choosing at least one or two to create consistently. Go with whatever feels most natural to you and where your ideal client hangs out.

Regardless of the format or channel, there are four things you need to talk about to get people to connect with your offer. These are the four messaging pillars that form a strong, stable structure for your business. Each one is an essential element of the value you bring to your customers' lives. Not every customer needs to be exposed to all four pillars before they decide to buy, but many do, and you never know which element will be the most compelling for a given person.

1. STORYTELLING AND EMOTION

This content calls out what the reader wants and educates them on how you give it to them. Help your audience become aware of their problem, understand the options for solving it, and see why your solution is the best fit for them. For example, Alexis (our sustainable jewelry designer) can talk about why jewelry is such an important part of a wardrobe, why she values keeping prices affordable, and how her use of sustainable materials benefits the planet. Anything that speaks to your ideal customer's needs and connects them to your brand fits in this messaging pillar.

2. EXPERT POSITIONING

This content establishes your authority in your niche and helps your audience feel comfortable buying from you. It should speak to both your experience and your personal brand; that is, the connection points people can relate to that may or may not have anything to do with your skill level. For example, Alexis might talk about the steps she takes to ensure her materials are eco-friendly, how she learned to make jewelry, and the value of hand-crafted pieces over mass-manufactured jewelry.

3. FOMO

(That's fear of missing out, in case you just woke up from a twenty-year coma.) Use testimonials, case studies, and product features to show off your work and generate desire. This can include customer quotes, stories about what they've gotten out of buying from you, pictures of the product in use or the results it can generate. Remember, if you want to use anyone else's words or images, ask permission first. Alexis could talk about how to style a new piece in five different ways for an upcoming holiday, share the story of a couple who hired her to design their engagement and wedding rings, or post meaningful testimonials that illustrate her value.

4. LOGISTICAL STUFF

These are the facts and figures of your offer. Tell your audience what they get when they buy from you, how to make the most of it, and how you support them after the purchase. Cover the basics, but also go beyond them to show your audience how you've anticipated their questions and concerns. Alexis would talk about things like the materials she uses, how to take care of her pieces, how to get a piece repaired or resized, or how to work with her on custom designs.

These four messaging pillars should appear in all your copywriting (that's just a fancy word for writing that's meant to sell something). However, that doesn't mean you should try to hit all four pillars every time you publish. Just focus on one pillar at a time as you're creating content, and change your focus for each new piece. Over time, a collection of your content on a given channel should include a pretty balanced distribution of all four.

Selling through content is a massive subject that could be an entire book by itself, and many smart people have already written that book. As with your personal brand, don't let perfection get in the way of starting. In the beginning, you don't need a complicated strategy. Don't spend weeks trying to learn how to do content marketing "right" when you could have spent that time actually creating content and watching what happens. Trial and error is a *great* teacher. Right now, all you need to do is make content that feels genuine and delivers what your customers want and need to hear from you, then put it in front of all the eyeballs you can reach.

That last part can be the most intimidating. Again, there are whole books (and blogs and courses and podcasts) on building your audience, and again, you don't need them yet. Just start with whatever audience you already have: family, friends, colleagues, your personal social accounts, and whatever else you already have access to. People often think they should start new social accounts for their business, but that forces you to start with zero followers. It's much easier and more productive to first use what you have instead of starting from scratch. Remember, the people in your circle already know, like, and trust you, so getting them to support you will be much easier than convincing someone who has never heard of you before.

Later, when you've gotten the hang of creating and sharing content, you can spend more time learning the intricacies of content marketing and audience building. But that's *not* step one—first you need to try it with what you already have available and see what happens. Then it doesn't become an obstacle to starting your business, and when you do invest time in up-leveling your content marketing game, you'll have a much clearer understanding of the problems and solutions that are relevant to you.

POSITION YOUR VALUE

Before we wrap up this chapter, I want to dedicate a little space to a big question that always comes up when I talk about messaging: how much should you charge?

As you can imagine, there's no single right answer. Prices vary enormously depending on your industry, your offer, and your position in the market. If this were an easy question, it wouldn't come up *so* often in Facebook groups and forums for entrepreneurs. Everyone who is new to selling their own products and services struggles with this, and it can take time to calibrate and get it right. What "right" even means is up for debate, since it depends on your goals for the business. So, I can't give you a straight answer, but I can guide you through a process that can help you arrive at a price that works well for you.

First, do your research to understand the standards in your market and how much demand exists. Shop around for other products and services like yours, and take note of the prices you see and the details of what you get for that price. Are certain deal structures common? For example, wedding photographers often have packages based on time, for example, a six-hour, eight-hour, or full-day package. Are discounts, coupons, or bundles common? For example, online retailers often give a coupon for your first order in exchange for signing up for their email list. Are businesses competing aggressively for customers, or is there plenty of demand to go around?

Now that you have the lay of the land, you need to decide where you stand in it. Take into account your experience, the quality you can provide, *and* how you want to be perceived. Remember that price is a signal—it tells people something about the quality and accessibility of your product before they ever experience it. A price that's too low can lead them to assume your quality is low, and if that's not what they want, they'll move along. If you're a newbie and feel that you need to start with lower prices to attract your first few customers, that's fair, but don't be shy about raising them once you've built up some credibility and expertise.

Also, don't forget to factor in your costs and your income goals as well. If you need to pay for raw materials, manufacturing, labor, transportation, equipment, marketing, rent, or other expenses, your prices need to cover those costs and still leave you with a healthy profit margin. And if there's a cap on how much work you can do—for instance, if you're selling your time rather than a scalable product—your prices should allow you to reach a reasonable income goal within the hours you have available for work.

The most important thing is to understand why your prices are set the way they are and to stand by them with confidence. It's inevitable that someone will challenge your pricing at some point. They'll say you're overcharging or ask for a discount, and in that moment, you need to be able to kindly but firmly educate them about why your work is worth what you're charging for it. If you're not convinced that your price is fair and well worth the value you deliver, you're inviting aggressive customers to walk all over you.

The best way to maintain that confidence is to overdeliver on the value of what you're selling. Improve your product or service until customers are so thrilled with the results that they'd be willing to pay even more than what you're charging. That's the kind of experience that leads people to tell all their friends and come back for more, and it will give you the strength to never compromise on your prices.

✳ ✳ ✳

Almost every space is crowded with lookalike businesses, especially online. Even more than what you do, what you *say* about what you do is the key to rising above the masses. Words are your most valuable marketing tool. They are the threads of connection between you and your ideal customer, and when you use them well, they do so much work for you. They attract the right people, raise their awareness of the problem you solve, communicate your value, build relationships, and more. Perfecting your messaging is a never-ending process because as long as you're in business, you'll be continuously improving your skills, evolving your offerings, and learning about your customers. With the work you've done in this chapter, you're off to a solid start, and starting is the hardest part.

In all the communication you'll be doing in your business, you won't always line up perfectly with the person on the other side of the conversation. Thankfully, that doesn't have to translate to conflict. Women have the skills to work through differences in a way that makes everyone feel like a winner, and in the next chapter, you'll learn how to use them in sales negotiations.

CHAPTER 5

TURN NEGOTIATION INTO COLLABORATION

When I gave up on my first business and got a job at a corporate gym, my feelings about sales went from bad to worse. At that point, I had already spent two frustrating years using ineffective, old-fashioned sales strategies and failing to understand why they weren't working. I was still ignorant of the new way of selling—emotional intelligence sales—that I've been teaching you in this book, and on top of that, I now had to conform to the gym's aggressive sales protocol.

As a personal trainer, part of my job was to sell personal training services, and we had quotas to meet. The gym's policy was to offer them to every new member, and not just as an option they could take or leave during the sign-up process. No, we had to cold call them after they'd joined the gym and try to talk them into it, regardless of whether they'd ever talked to a trainer before or expressed any interest in personal training. The gym's view was that everyone needed personal training—they just didn't know it yet, and it was our job to push them into it.

Most of the time, those calls ended with a firm "No, thank you" or *click* (*crickets*). If I managed to convince someone to come into the gym to discuss it further, they showed up armed to resist instead of excited to learn more. That was totally understandable, since none of it was their idea in the first place, so there was no intrinsic motivation to see it through. It made me feel like a villain, so I'd just power through the spiel and hope to get it all over with quickly. The answer was usually no, which made perfect sense because they had no reason to trust that I had their best interests at heart.

Once we got to this point, there was virtually no possibility of a productive negotiation. Not only did I have no flexibility on the offer (since it wasn't my business), but I also had no standing to respond to their objections in a believable way. If they said the cost was too high, they didn't have the time, or didn't think it would make a difference in their results, who was I to argue? I was clearly out to sell, and no one likes to be sold to. Any further explanations or arguments on my part just sounded desperate and manipulative (because they were).

These unpleasant conversations irrevocably tainted the customer's experience of the gym. They felt annoyed that the gym treated them like a wallet, and they avoided me and the other trainers because they didn't want to get pitched to. Instead of being a helpful and energizing presence in the gym, I became an adversary, all because of masculine-style negotiation tactics.

In this old (and useless) way of negotiating, the goal is to win at all costs. So, it's probably not surprising that manipulation, aggression, and dishonesty are typical parts of this process. The result is a combative interaction with the customer that lays a shaky foundation for any ongoing relationship after you get the result you want. If you've ever given in to something and walked away wondering if you'd made a huge mistake, you were a victim of this kind of negotiation.

Lots of people, especially women, avoid negotiation because they think the only way to win is to be pushy, and the only alternative is to take no for an answer. In reality, the "us against them" mentality is a fallacy. People want to feel seen, heard, and understood, and that's as true in sales negotiations as in any other conversation. Even though I was constrained to a certain extent at the gym, there were plenty of things I could have done to make those negotiations feel a lot better and leave the door open for a no to become a yes later. With the right approach to negotiation, you can make anyone feel like you're on their team, which will make them happy to buy from you.

THREE STEPS TO SOLVE PROBLEMS TOGETHER

For some people, just the word *negotiation* is enough to bring up intimidating visions of big-money business deals, high-stakes hostage situations, and tense plea bargains. Relax—I wouldn't get near that stuff with a ten-foot pole. Our negotiations are nothing more than handling objections, a.k.a. all the reasons your customers give for not saying yes to your offer.

Done right, negotiations feel like normal, pleasant conversations, and they can deepen instead of destroy your relationship with a customer. This simple three-step process will guide you to respond to their concerns in a way that makes them feel like you're working toward the same goal together. Not only will it help you get to yes more often, but it will also make that yes more enthusiastic and leave a no more open to becoming a yes later.

STEP 1: VALIDATE THEIR FEELINGS.

Whenever a customer expresses hesitation or concern about your offer, the first thing you need to do is show your understanding of their view. Acknowledge that you hear them and explain that it's perfectly normal and ok to react that way. Let them know that other customers often have similar concerns or that you get that question all the time, if that's true. When people resist your offer, your instinct might be to resist their resistance (*No, don't say no!*), and that's what leads to an adversarial situation. Nip this in the bud by accepting and validating their feelings instead.

STEP 2: CLARIFY THE OBJECTION.

Next, find out what's really bothering them. Don't take a no emotionally or at face value—people often don't say right away what they're really thinking. Instead, dig deeper in a way that's loving and curious by asking more questions. Below are three of the most common objections and how you can get to the heart of that concern.

"I need to think about it."

This catchall phrase can obscure all kinds of concerns, so don't let the conversation end there. Ask them to explain what's weighing on their mind and say that you'd like to answer all their questions while you're there to help. Emphasize that you want to help them make the right decision for them (and mean it!).

"I don't have the time."

Ideally, this is something your marketing content should address before someone gets to a serious sales conversation with you. Your messaging can show them the value of investing their time in your solution, and it should help them decide whether now is the right moment to do it. That said, when this objection comes up, there are two questions to ask. First, are they willing to make time for something that's important to them? The answer is nearly always yes. If it is, then do they honestly not know how to make the time, or is there another reason they're afraid to commit? For example, lack of time is sometimes an excuse for lack of self-accountability—they might be scared that *they* won't take it seriously enough to get the results they want.

"I don't have the money."

To avoid running into this objection too often, it's crucial to prequalify customers on the investment level multiple times before you speak with them. If you don't list all your prices openly (which is common for high-ticket offerings), consider including a starting price on your website or contact form. In that same form, ask what their budget is or whether they are ready to invest in themselves. Then, if this objection comes up in your conversation, clarify where it's coming from. Do they feel the value they're getting doesn't justify the price, or do they have a fixed budget for this that they simply can't go over?

STEP 3: DECIDE WHETHER TO EDUCATE OR CUSTOMIZE.

Once you understand where an objection is coming from, there are two options for addressing it. You can educate the customer, which involves explaining (in a way that directly relates to their concerns) how you provide value and why it's worth the investment. Alternatively, you can customize the offer so that it better fits their needs, as long as the change doesn't compromise the integrity of your business or make you uncomfortable. Which one you choose depends entirely on the circumstances and your judgment, so I'll describe a couple of scenarios to illustrate what you can do.

Example 1

Jasmine sells high-quality organic children's clothing, and she's talking to a mom who wants to buy matching shirts for her triplets, but the price for all three is too steep. If the mom is a previous customer and Jasmine values her avid supporters, she might offer a buy-two-get-one-free coupon. This would make the customer feel like she's getting a win and the owner is doing her a favor, which could motivate her to spread the word about the brand. If Jasmine would rather not discount her prices, she can explain that the price supports the value the customer cares about—the eco-friendly materials, durable stitching, and unique designs. She can point out that the customer's kids will get more use out of these shirts because they'll love the design, and the shirt won't fall apart as quickly as a cheap one would. Plus, if the customer finds a defect in quality within six months, she can get a free replacement.

Example 2

Brianna, a wedding photographer, is talking to a couple who is hesitating at the $3,500 price tag of the eight-hour standard package. Usually, Brianna takes a 50 percent deposit and collects the rest thirty days before the wedding, but she could make the package more accessible by offering a flexible payment plan. A lower down payment and smaller installments over time may be easier on the couple's budget and less scary than big chunks of money. Alternatively, she could emphasize that the wedding photos will be the one thing they'll have to remember the day after it's over. They'll be looking at those photos on their walls, phones, and computers every single day, and the last thing they want is disappointing photos that remind them of a subpar experience with the photographer. It's worth making the investment to get a result they'll be happy with on the big day and for the rest of their lives.

When deciding whether to educate or customize, consider both the customer's motives and your own comfort level. Sometimes, being flexible is a great way to help someone out without sacrificing much of anything, and those customers are often especially grateful and loyal because you were willing to make it work for them. However, explaining the value of your offer can be just as powerful, and it's much better to do that than change your offer in a way that compromises the value or makes you uncomfortable.

TROUBLESHOOT WITH THE THREE STEPS

There are a few ways that sales negotiations commonly go sideways. Fortunately, using the three steps you just learned will prevent or fix all of them. Let me show you what I mean.

PROBLEM 1: YOU DON'T NEGOTIATE AT ALL.

This is what nice people do when they believe the only way to negotiate is to be pushy or manipulative. They opt out and take the first no for an answer: "Ok, sounds good, let me know if you change your mind!" If you do this, you give up the opportunity to get to the bottom of the objection, which puts you at a disadvantage in two ways. First, you don't know why they really said no, so you can't make any improvements to your offer based on their feedback. Second, you haven't built a rapport with the person, so they're unlikely to ever come back and turn that no into a yes in the future.

The solution is simple: use the three steps! Even if they don't get you to yes this time, you'll have learned something and deepened a relationship with a potential customer.

PROBLEM 2: YOU DON'T KNOW WHEN TO STOP.

One of the worst negotiation experiences from the customer's perspective is when the seller doesn't know when to stop selling and accept the no. Listening is at the core of each of the three steps, and if you're truly listening, you'll know when a no is definitive.

If the customer is giving you a hard no right off the bat, you know you need to do a better job of qualifying prospects before you invest time in talking to them one-on-one. Same if they don't want to reveal their true objections or seem to be making excuses—that's a sign that you need to do a better job of educating prospects about the investment or commitment through your content. If they still say no after you explain your value or offer a custom solution, it may just be the wrong time for them. In that case, let them go but stay in touch because this type of person is more likely to come back to the offer in the future.

PROBLEM 3: YOU BEND OVER BACKWARD TO GET THE SALE.

This can be tempting, especially at first, when you don't have many customers. DON'T DO IT. If you win the sale this way, you lose in the long run because you'll be stuck with a demanding customer who expects you to give in to every ask and wants to squeeze all the value out of you. When you break your boundaries for a customer, it's extremely difficult to put them back up again without upsetting them, and upset customers can have real negative impacts on your brand's reputation. Plus, you won't enjoy the work because you'll know you're not being compensated or appreciated the way you should be.

Preventing this problem comes down to standing your ground in Step 3. Steer clear of major discounts, highly customized packages, or exceptions to your standard processes. When in doubt, just stay firm in your offer. If they say no, you'll have dodged a bullet, and if they say yes, they'll be more likely to respect your boundaries and value your work.

NURTURE THE RELATIONSHIP

I've said it before, and here it comes again: sales is a numbers game. You won't always get to yes, and it's ok because your offer isn't right for everyone. That's by design. You built your business for your ideal customer, so if some other people come along and don't see the value for them, it just means they're not your ideal customer. There's no need to take it personally—it just wasn't the right fit for them.

That said, a no now isn't necessarily a no forever. If someone took the time to consume your content, reach out to you, and have a conversation with you, *something* about your offer connected with them. Maybe the circumstances weren't right for them to make the purchase at that time, but circumstances change, and your offerings might change too. If you keep the lead warm by following up and engaging with them through social media or email, you'll maximize the chances that their no becomes a yes one day.

If you do get to yes, make sure you set the right expectations for what happens next. The more transparent you are about how you do business, the less likely you'll end up with an angry or disappointed customer down the line. For example, if you sell products, what's your refund or return policy? If you provide services, how do you communicate with clients and manage the logistics? What do customers need to know to get the most value from their purchase and avoid problems? What can they expect from you and when?

Essentially, you want to pave the way for the best possible customer relationships. A good way to do this is to imagine your worst-case scenarios. Could someone get hurt using your products or services? Damage their property? Lose business or income? Are you making any claims or promises that you can't guarantee? Of course, you need to protect yourself legally against the possibility of being held liable for any of those outcomes. But it's just as important to protect yourself by setting the right expectations for your customers and supporting them when problems inevitably arise.

* * *

In every sales conversation, the goal is to make both parties feel like they made an empowered decision, even if agreement wasn't the end result. It doesn't take complicated strategizing or advanced negotiation skills to make this happen. All you need to do is follow three simple steps whenever an objection comes up: validate their feelings, clarify the objection, and decide whether to educate or customize. If you listen to understand (not to respond) and stay focused on solving the customer's problem (not making the sale), this process works like magic.

Thinking back to my cold-calling days at the gym, I couldn't be more grateful to the people who taught me what I've shared with you in this chapter. If that were the only way to do business, you can be damn sure I would never have become the entrepreneur I am today. Back then, most sales appointments made me want to walk right out of that gym and never look back. Now, I get excited to talk to potential customers because I know it can lead to a win-win transaction and the beginning of a beautiful relationship.

The last four chapters have taught you the basic skills you'll need as an entrepreneur, but you're not a master yet. The most powerful shortcut to mastery is *other people*. Not just anyone—you need people who can give you relevant feedback, emotional support, and useful advice. The next chapter will tell you how to find them.

CHAPTER 6

FIND YOUR PEOPLE

When I first started my business, I was all alone. I didn't know anyone doing anything like this—no entrepreneurial uncles, no high school or college buddies jumping on the online business bandwagon. My family was always supportive, for which I'm eternally grateful, but they couldn't help me actually figure out what to do or how to do it. The only feedback I got was from my clients, and while it was important to know whether they were happy with my work, they obviously couldn't help me advance as a professional—I was already the expert in the room for them.

And then socially, I felt more alone than ever. All my friends from high school were taking the traditional route to college and career, and they had no understanding or sympathy for what I was dealing with. I tried to convince myself that I was imagining this subtle superiority complex they seemed to have developed, but I realized that it was all too real one day when I met an old friend for lunch. I was telling her about my experience, venting about people who gave me this attitude that I was less than them because they're in college or in the corporate world. She laughed and said something like, "Yeah...except that I have an engineering degree, which is actually better." Yikes (*unfriend*).

I always had that hypercritical voice in the back of my mind, and it damaged more than just my mood and ego. Since I wasn't fully focused on my customers, the quality of my work suffered. So did my judgment, with my inner critic second-guessing every little decision. No one was congratulating me or encouraging me, so maybe I really *was* making a mistake.

This miserable mental state only changed when I started surrounding myself with other entrepreneurs. It started with the job that saved me from the unbearable corporate gym, when a successful fitness influencer hired me after I connected with her on social media. I started reaching out more, contributing to online conversations, and attending local events about fitness and entrepreneurship. Making friends who shared these interests turned out to be a lot easier than I thought, and suddenly I had people in my life who could teach me, push me, and encourage me to keep at it on the tough days. They still do, and without them I absolutely wouldn't be here, in my dream house, running a business I love and writing this book for you.

It's easier and more common than ever to work in isolation. If you're running an online business, you can do it all from home. It seems like you can get all the information and skills you need just by consuming online content from YouTube University, and when you need help, you can just hire a freelancer on the web. In theory, you could run your business without ever leaving your house or interacting with anyone besides your customers and vendors.

In reality, though, that doesn't mean you should. As I learned the hard way, making yourself an island is a great way to stall and burn out. So, don't go at it alone. The journey will be much easier if you surround yourself with other people who are striving for (or have achieved) the same goals as you.

WHY YOU NEED A SUPPORT NETWORK

No one achieves great things all on their own. Social support is essential for men and women alike, and research has shown that people who have strong relationships have less stress and fewer health problems than people who feel isolated.[13] On a professional level, strong networks provide information and advice, access to opportunities, and valuable feedback on your work. Close professional relationships offer the best of both worlds. They motivate you to work hard,

---

13 "Manage Stress: Strengthen Your Support Network," American Psychological Association, last modified October 8, 2019, https://www.apa.org/topics/stress/manage-social-support.

help you level up your skills, and cheerlead you when the going gets tough.

The problem is that women are more likely to encounter barriers to building them and reaping the benefits.[14] As in other male-dominated fields, female entrepreneurs have a harder time finding peers and role models we can relate to. Plus, our male counterparts often don't face the same challenges we do, especially when it comes to issues like taking care of a family and defying social expectations.[15] For that reason, having a close inner "work" circle is even more critical for your success than it would be for a man.[16] Unfortunately, it also means you're more likely to end up feeling isolated in your work and miss out on the benefits of strong connections with people who share your entrepreneurial goals.

That's why I couldn't let this book end without devoting a chapter to helping you build the supportive network you need. Women value community—we don't want to feel alone and do it all ourselves. But when you're starting a business, there are no coworkers to chat with or office happy hours

14 Virginia Gewin, "Women Can Benefit from Female-Led Networks," *Nature*, December 20, 2018, https://www.nature.com/articles/d41586-018-07878-w.

15 Paula Fernandes and Marisa Sanfilippo, "Challenges Faced by Women Entrepreneurs and Some of the Most Successful Women to Follow," *Business News Daily*, June 11, 2020, https://www.businessnewsdaily.com/5268-women-entrepreneur-challenges.html.

16 Brian Uzzi, "Research: Men and Women Need Different Kinds of Networks to Succeed," *Harvard Business Review*, February 25, 2019, https://hbr.org/2019/02/research-men-and-women-need-different-kinds-of-networks-to-succeed.

to introduce you to new people, so it's all too easy to put networking on the back burner indefinitely.

You're just a few clicks away from millions and millions of people, but that abundance can make it feel even harder to find what you're looking for. It's like walking into a massive festival and looking for your friends—you'll have a hard time finding them unless you know what to look for and where they're likely to hang out. I can't answer that definitively for you, but I can give you some guidance to help you figure out the answer for yourself.

MAKE FRIENDS, NOT CONTACTS

Don't think of this process as building a professional network. That sounds like shaking hands and collecting business cards from people in suits drinking fancy cocktails. Whether that sounds like your idea of a good time or a nightmare, that type of connection is too superficial to do you much good. Yes, weak ties like those can be good for sourcing opportunities, but would you send them an S.O.S. text when you're having a bad day? Not so much.

That's why your goal should be to make friends—bona fide, got-your-back friends who will give you feedback without the sugar coating and come to your rescue when it's all too much. Of course, this won't happen instantly. That kind of closeness takes time, even when you hit it off with someone right away. But aiming to make friends rather than "build a network" from the very beginning will make that goal easier to achieve. The choices you'll make about where to look, how to reach out, and what to do after the first conversation will all be more likely to lead to meaningful relationships that will make a difference in your business and your life.

Since you're looking to make friends and not to get ahead, aim for people who are doing what you're doing, at the level you're doing it. Don't try to reach out to mega-influencers, celebrity entrepreneurs, and other people who are way ahead of where you are. Even if they're kind enough to respond, that sort of unbalanced relationship doesn't fit the bill. They'd be more like your professor than your friend, and have you ever called up a professor to say you're having a bad day? I didn't think so.

There are so many groups, events, and online hangouts for entrepreneurs that it can be tough to know where to go to find people you'll genuinely want to spend time with. After all, as you've learned from this book, not all entrepreneurs have the same idea of what it means to run a business well. Where will you find someone whose approach, industry, and personality have something in common with yours?

The best shortcut is to look for shared role models. If you love a certain blog, podcast, or book about business, check out the person who made it and see if they run an online community (often a Facebook group), teach courses, or do in-person events. If they do, get involved. Other people who love what you love are way more likely to be grade-A friend material than someone in a random forum or meetup group for entrepreneurs. A similar approach is to look for shared values. For example, a Facebook group or weekend workshop for "heart-centered entrepreneurs" is a good bet if that's how you would describe yourself. You'll walk in (or log in) knowing you have that in common with everyone else there.

How many friends is enough? The closer the relationships are, the fewer you need. Even just two or three great friends who share your business goals and values can make a massive difference in your success and the quality of your life. More isn't necessarily better—having too many outside opinions coming at you can be confusing and distracting. However, that doesn't mean you should stop socializing once you've got two friends in the bag. Keep in mind that there may be a lot of misses before you get hits, and you may outgrow people over time. That's normal, and it's also a good reason to keep regularly participating in a wider community beyond your close friends.

LOCAL VS. ONLINE

Great friendships can bloom from local or online connections, but each medium has its advantages and disadvantages. Personally, I've gotten massive value from both, so I always recommend that you give both a try, even if your first instinct is to stick with one or the other. If nothing else, it's good practice for expanding the limits of your comfort zone, which you'll have to do many times as you build and improve your business.

Local connections are valuable because in-person interactions are much richer than online ones, especially when you're first meeting someone. You know what I mean— there's massive power in looking someone in the eye, shaking their hand, hearing their voice, and seeing their body language. Not to mention that the conversation has to flow in the moment, not drip along one message at a time, getting interrupted by a thousand other things. That's why you should look for local workshops, conferences, classes, meetups, and other in-person events related to what you do. You can find them by searching online, and those searches will often lead to local event calendars or relevant organizations (like universities or community centers) you can follow to find out about future events.

While it's much easier to start a friendship this way, the opportunities are more limited and less convenient than they are online. If you live in a major metropolitan area and have the means and time to get yourself to an in-person gathering, these limitations aren't too onerous. But if your community is small or it's hard for you to get around, attending a relevant in-person event can be a major challenge. In that case, looking for online connections might be your best bet. If you can, though, I would still try to attend an in-person event occasionally, even if it's just once a year and you have to travel for it. Is there an amazing annual conference or retreat for people like you that you're dying to go to? Save up your vacation time to make it happen, and if you can't afford it financially, reach out to the organizers to see if they have a scholarship or volunteer program that would reduce your costs.

The internet offers easy access to a huge number of people, but it can be harder to form meaningful and lasting relationships. It's not impossible, though. If you're consistent, genuine, and sensitive to other people's vibes, you can find amazing friends online—kindred souls who you otherwise might never have met. In fact, one of my bridesmaids at my wedding in 2019 was a friend I met online two years prior!

One way is to participate in communities like Facebook groups, virtual meetups, forums, and chat rooms dedicated to people like you. As mentioned before, communities hosted by your favorite business or industry influencers are a great place to start because they're bound to be full of like-minded people. That's not the only option, though. Just hop on a search engine and type in "online community for entrepreneurs" or replace "entrepreneurs" with something more specific, like "web designers" or "personal chefs" or whatever it is that you do. You're bound to find something. When you do, take a look around to get a sense for whether it's a good fit for you. Read the description and the rules, browse a few posts, and make sure you can see yourself enjoying the conversations and spending time getting to know these people. If you like what you see, join up and introduce yourself.

Another way to make connections online is one-on-one through social media, whether it's Instagram (my personal favorite), Facebook, Twitter, Pinterest, LinkedIn, or any other platform. Remember, a huge part of what you'll do to grow your business is post content online and engage with the people who consume it. So, you can find other people like you by consuming their content and engaging with them. Start by browsing content related to what you do. When you find a post that grabs your attention, check out that person's profile to see if they seem like a good potential friend (i.e., they're doing what you're doing at the level you're doing it). If the answer is yes, follow them and either comment on their post or respond to a story. Treat it like a real live conversation—say what you liked about it, share your perspective on the topic, and ask a question to keep the conversation going.

FREE VS. PAID

Plenty of social opportunities online and in the real world are free. Free is good, right? Well, yes and no. The good part is that you can test multiple places to see which is the right fit, and if you decide to leave, you haven't invested anything but your time. Plus, free groups and events tend to be bigger, so it feels like they offer more possible friends to connect with. In reality, though, free opportunities are usually only effective for connecting on a very basic level, and it usually requires a lot more effort to turn those superficial connections into meaningful friendships.

One reason for this is that managing a community or event takes time and effort, which are valuable assets. If membership is free, there's probably not much management going on at all (hello, spammers and trolls). That makes for a sucky experience, and anyone who's looking to build strong, authentic relationships is probably not going to stick around long. So despite the thousands of people you might encounter there, your chances of making a lasting friend are not so hot.

Another reason free opportunities are usually low quality is that there's no incentive for participants to make it great. When you pay for something, you take it more seriously. You've made an investment and are motivated to get value out of it, so you'll participate more, and so will all the other people who paid to be there. By requiring that investment, the group keeps out the lurkers and dabblers who bring down the quality of the discussion and distract from what really matters. Higher engagement leads to more and better conversations, even though the number of people involved may be smaller.

In addition to putting you in touch with a high-quality group of potential friends, opportunities that cost money usually provide valuable education that will give your business a massive boost. Conferences, workshops, courses, coaching groups, mastermind groups, and gated professional organizations all put a big chunk of your fees toward providing helpful content. For me, in-person business retreats and conferences are always game changers that turn my mindset and business around completely. Plus, they introduce me to people who become invaluable friends and mentors.

If you're considering something like that, don't wait until later. It can be tempting to say that you'll do it in a few months or next year, when you've got your feet under you with this whole business thing. You'll get more out of it if you already have some experience to go on, right? Wrong. Think about it—if you wanted to learn guitar, should you fumble around on your own for a year and *then* hire a teacher to undo all the bad habits and misconceptions you've picked up? Of course not. It would be much better to learn it the right way from the beginning because strong fundamentals would enable you to improve faster and keep learning on your own. At one event that I went to over *two years* after I started my business, my first thought was how much struggle and heartbreak I would have saved if I'd done it earlier.

MAKING IT LAST

I've given you a lot of advice about how to find your people, but that only gets you halfway there. You still have to build lasting friendships with the people you meet. There are no rules for how to do this, but as with any relationship, you get what you give. Treat people like people, not resources for your benefit, and approach every conversation with curiosity, authenticity, and a willingness to be vulnerable and share about yourself.

Not everyone will reciprocate, so when someone does, don't let it go to waste. Keep the relationship alive with regular communication and find creative ways to take it beyond the context where it began, whether that was online or in person. Here are some strategies that have worked well for me and the women that I coach:

- Message each other a few times a week
- Set up a weekly hangout call
- Have a coffee or lunch date
- Co-work together for a day
- Organize a group outing
- Go to a conference or other event together

If you live too far apart to get together in person, take these ideas virtual. A video call isn't as good as a face-to-face meeting, but it's a lot better than just words on a screen. Big events like conferences are the perfect opportunity to meet far-flung friends in person because you can all travel to one place, and rather than it being just a social call, it's a professional development opportunity that you can all share together.

* * *

Just like the business skills you learned in previous chapters, building a strong support network takes time, but there's nothing keeping you from starting now. The first step is simple: reach out. Make it a regular task, just like brushing your teeth or checking your email. As your connections evolve into friendships, the form of outreach changes, but the need to do it consistently doesn't. If you keep at it, those relationships will enrich your life and move your business forward faster than you ever could have on your own.

CONCLUSION

In 2017, two rocky years after I had started my online fitness coaching business, I finally got on the right track. It was like the blinds were lifted and I could finally see that the problem wasn't me, it was my *behavior*. I had been doing all the wrong things, but that didn't mean I wasn't cut out for entrepreneurship—it just meant that if I wanted to succeed, I had to value my problems enough to fix them. After surrounding myself with advanced entrepreneurs and getting on the fast track to mastering their skills, I sold $150K of my boss's online programs in less than a year. Once I got that taste for success, there was no going back.

Within half a year of doing sales for others, I felt confident in what I was doing and decided to relaunch my own online business. It started with fitness coaching, but I quickly pivoted to fill the gap of teaching other women the sales process

I had mastered. Finally, after struggling and hustling for so long, it felt like the pieces were falling into place. I built a steady flow of customers who were willing to pay premium prices for the value I provided to them, and that allowed me to do more than just sell and coach all day long. I had space to step back and make intentional choices about how to invest my time and energy, which enabled the business to grow even faster.

Since then, I've balanced working *in* the business with working *on* it. Working in the business means doing the day-to-day work of attracting and serving customers, which for me includes things like coaching clients, creating content, engaging with followers on social media, and doing sales calls. That's essential stuff, but if it's all you do, you're bound to hit a ceiling at some point. To keep thriving, you also need to work on the business, which means taking the time to think about how you can do things better and grow.

There's always room to improve your offering, your messaging, your branding, your website, and your sales process. In the beginning, optimizing those customer-facing marketing elements is usually the top priority. As you grow, your attention will likely shift toward improving your back-end systems for handling tasks like logistics and finances. Regardless of the stage of your business, never forget to keep investing in your own continuous development, both in your craft and as an entrepreneur. I still spend several hours a week on some kind of learning, whether it's self-directed education, collaboration with others, or development of my team members' skills.

At some point, you may want to hire people to help you, whether they're project-based contractors or full employees. I work with several contractors regularly, including a graphic designer, web developer, photographer, and executive assistant, but I have yet to hire my first employee. That's by design—I like having a business that I can run almost entirely on my own. A lot of the cultural narrative around entrepreneurship is focused on rapid, massive growth, but that comes with serious risks and responsibilities. You can make a big impact and a great living even if your company is just you, and that's an option that works well for lots of entrepreneurs.

It's been three years since my business took off, and I'm only twenty-five years old. I never expected to be living my dream life so soon, but running a business isn't like climbing the corporate ladder, where you have to wait years for each promotion. When you take your dreams (and income) into your own hands, hitting your goals doesn't have to be a far-fetched idea that's off in the distant future. To set your business up for long-term success, all it takes is consistently doing the right things over time. As you know by now, I wasn't naturally gifted at entrepreneurship, and I haven't used some secret sauce or caught a lucky break that suddenly sent my business skyrocketing. Once I learned the fundamental ideas and skills I've shared with you in this book, I applied them every single day, adjusting my tactics as I learned more about my customers and my industry.

Looking to the future, I know I'll never stop adjusting. Change is nonnegotiable, in business as in life, and you have to stay flexible if you want your business to thrive long-term. People often ask if that scares me, and truly the answer is no. I know I have all the tools to start another business at the drop of the hat if I need to. These strategies are time-tested and proven to work, so I can set myself up for success again and again no matter what, and if you invest the time to master the skills in this book, you can too. Now, after just a couple of good years in business, I'm already looking into expanding into other streams of income, building more businesses, and creating generational wealth.

I'm not saying any of this to brag, intimidate, or make you think this is easy. I'm encouraging you to aim high and do the work. If you do, results can happen quicker than you ever imagined. Look at me—I've always been in competitive industries (fitness and online business), and I don't have any wildly special qualifications in either one. But there are a lot of people I can help, and I make sure that the ones who will learn best from me can find me. Most importantly, I do it in a way that feels good for both me and my customers, building an emotional connection that leads to satisfaction, loyalty, and results for both of us.

That's exactly what you've just learned to do. First, you recognized and threw out the innocent-looking but poisonous myths that were standing between you and your business dreams. Then you began to own your authority by recognizing the value you have to offer others and taking deliberate steps to move further along the spectrum of expertise in your craft. You learned to harness your natural emotional intelligence to connect deeply with your customers and guide them toward the solution that's right for them. Next, you discovered how to craft compelling messaging that attracts your ideal customer and prepares them to buy from you. You saw how to turn negotiation into collaboration by working with the customer to solve their problem instead of working to close the sale. And finally, you came to understand the importance of a supportive social circle and how to build one of your own.

Now, it's time to get off your butt and put all that good stuff to use. I invite you to a thirty-day challenge with three goals. First, show up on social media every day. Post something, respond to someone, and start engaging with potential customers and other people in your industry. Second, take two small steps toward your business goals every day. There are so many little things to do, from choosing a name to crafting your offer, so don't let the day end without ticking two items (however small) off the list. Third, bring money in the door before the thirty days are up. Until you start making money, your business is just a hobby, so don't let it stay that way for long. Make at least one sale this month to get the ball rolling (I promise you can do this no matter how "crazy" it may sound).

Starting a business can seem scary, even after you've gotten an inside view of how it works. Just remember that everything begins with baby steps, and if you take them consistently, you'll be making real progress before you know it. You were born to do this—women are biologically and socially primed to connect with other people, and at its core, that's what business is. That's one half of the equation, and if you've made it all the way to the end of this book, you know the other half—the dream and the desire to see it through—is there too. *You got this.* Now, go make it happen.

ACKNOWLEDGMENTS

Writing this book was truly a labor of love and so fulfilling for me, although doing it while pregnant with my second baby was much harder than I thought it would be. Having a supportive team around me is the only reason I was able to conquer this challenge and get my words out and into the hands of the masses.

I'm eternally grateful to my husband, Kyle, as well as my mom, Dawn, and my sister, April, who have both been the biggest supporters of me and my business since day one. You all have gone above and beyond to help propel my success, and there is absolutely no way I could have made it this far without your encouragement.

Also, a very special thanks goes to my online community, who sparked the idea for this book and inspired me to write it. Thank you for putting your faith in me as a leader and teacher for the sales community. Your trust is something I never take for granted, and I hope I did it justice.

Writing a book is a giant undertaking, and to everyone at Scribe Media who contributed to creating this book and helping it come alive, thank you so much. Specifically my Publishing Manager, Neddie Ann, and my Scribe, Madison— you two have been such an integral piece of the puzzle, I'm so grateful for all your time and help!

ABOUT THE AUTHOR

KARRIE BRADY is a seven-figure entrepreneur and an online educator passionate about putting more money in the hands of women everywhere. Dedicated to making the world of entrepreneurship more accessible to her clients, Karrie has helped thousands of women build an online business according to their own rules, personalities, and preferences. At just twenty-five, Karrie has appeared in *Forbes, Authority Magazine,* and *Medium* and been featured with Thrive Global and Create & Cultivate. She lives in Los Angeles with her husband, their two kids, and three rescue dogs. For more information, visit karriebrady.com.